Practical Pre-School

The Early Years Foundation Stage
in practice

by Liz Wilcock

Contents

Illustrated by Cathy Hughes

The views expressed in this book are those of the author.

Published by Step Forward Publishing Limited Tel: 020 7738 5454 www.practicalpreschool.com

The Early Years Foundation Stage *in practice* ISBN 978 1 904 575 276

Introduction

The Early Years Foundation Stage document (published April 2007) will come into force from September 2008.

The document brings together three existing documents that practitioners currently use –

■ The National Standards of Care for Under 8's in Day-care and Childminding

■ The Birth to Three Framework

■ The Curriculum Guidance for the Foundation Stage.

So, why has this happened? Why are we now being presented with, what many will regard as a 'new' document, to familiarise ourselves with?

It is, of course, widely acknowledged that every child deserves the best possible start in life. Experiences in the early years will have an important impact on future life opportunities. We all have a responsibility in ensuring that each child can be helped to reach his/her potential.

Lord Laming's report into the death of Victoria Climbie had recommendations that led to the publication of the Every Child Matters document. The Laming Report highlighted the problems between Social Services, the police and the NHS in supporting and protecting the most vulnerable of children in our society.

Following the proposals set out by the Government for changing the way in which children's services needed to be delivered nationally, a new system for inspection was introduced for day care settings. The intention was to ensure that children remained protected from harm and that each child could be supported to reach his/her full potential.

'We need to ensure we properly protect children at risk within a framework of universal services which support every child to develop to their full potential and which aim to prevent negative outcomes'.

The aim was for children and young people under the age of 19 years to reach their potential through a set of five outcomes. Nationally, children and young people were consulted about what matters most to them, and the five outcomes were the result of the consultation.

Being Healthy – what does this mean?
Enjoying good physical and mental health and living a healthy lifestyle.

Staying safe – what does this mean?
Being protected from harm and neglect.

Enjoying and achieving – what does this mean?
Getting the most out of life and developing the skills for adulthood.

Making a positive contribution – what does this mean?
Being involved with the community and society and not engaging in anti social or offending behaviour.

Economic well-being – what does this mean?
Not being prevented by economic disadvantage from achieving their full potential in life.

It was expected that all children's services nationally would work together to support each child individually. Early intervention at the onset of any problems for a child, means that action can be taken for the child and their family to receive the help and support they may need locally. It is a crucial part of Every Child Matters that agencies work together to act in the best interests of all children and their families, by improving the way in which information is shared. Each local authority has an appointed person to ensure that information is collected and shared with the relevant people. Local Safeguarding Boards have now been introduced within each local authority.

Following the publication of Every Child Matters the government passed the Children Act 2004, which had a clear focus around the needs of children, young people and families.

The Ten Year Childcare Strategy (2004) introduced the sector to 4 key themes –

1. Allowing parents choice and flexibility about balancing work and family life

2. Availability of high quality, affordable, flexible childcare places for all families of children aged up to 14 years to meet demand

3. High quality provision with a highly skilled childcare and early years workforce

4. Affordability for flexible, high quality childcare, appropriate for the individual child's needs.

Local authorities were issued with guidance to help them to plan for the new agenda.

In 2006, the Childcare Act came into force. The Act takes forward the key themes from the Ten Year Childcare Strategy to help transform early years services. In summary, the Act has four parts –

1. Duties on Local Authorities in England

2. Duties on Local Authorities in Wales

3. Regulation and inspection arrangements for childcare providers in England

4. General provisions.

The Act requires local authorities to improve the outcomes for all children up to the age of 5 years. Local authorities are required to assess the local childcare market and to secure sufficient childcare for working parents. Local authorities are not expected to provide childcare directly, but are expected to work with local private, voluntary and independent settings to meet the need. Local authorities are also expected to secure a free minimum amount of care and early learning for all 3 and 4 year olds whose parents want it.

Local authorities are required to provide parents with information about how they can access services they may need for their children up to the age of 20 years. The Act also introduced the Early Years Foundation Stage, which is described as a new framework supporting providers in the delivery of integrated care and early years education from birth – five years. The focus is on raising quality and standards.

The Early Years Register (EYR)

Providers who are currently registered with Ofsted will be transferred to the EYR. Settings will be registered who take children from birth – the 31st August following the child's 5th birthday. Private and voluntary providers using premises on a school site will be required to register on the EYR.

From September 2008, providers will be inspected by Ofsted under sections 49 and 50 of the Childcare Act 2006. Ofsted will give regard to the EYFS for the inspections. With the exception of schools, all settings will be required to register with Ofsted in respect of the their provision for children from birth to the end of the EYFS.

Provision in schools for registered pupils aged three and over will not be required to be register under EYFS because it is already taken account of by the main school inspection framework. It will, however, be expected to meet the same standards as other providers. All settings will be regularly inspected against the EYFS requirements and all provision made directly by schools will be inspected as part of a single inspection event with the main school inspection. Maintained, independent and non maintained special schools will be required to register only in respect of any provision they offer for children below the age of three years. This is to ensure extra safeguards for the youngest and most vulnerable of children.

The Childcare Register has two parts, compulsory (from September 2008) and voluntary (from April 2007). The compulsory part of the register is for providers who offer care to children from the end of the foundation stage up to the age of 8 years. The voluntary part of the register is for providers who

have not been previously been able to register with Ofsted. These include, for example, people who care for children in their own home (such as nannies), people who only offer care for children aged 8 years and over, and people who offer activity based provision (such as sports clubs).

The registers are new to most people. If you are unsure about which register applies to your setting, contact Ofsted on their help line number (08456 404040) or go to the Ofsted website to receive information and guidance. You local authority will have information on the EYR register and the Childcare registers too.

So, what does this mean for the practitioner?

The introduction of the Early Years Foundation Stage (EYFS) is likely to cause some initial anxiety. People have stated that the last thing we need now is yet 'another document' to work with. National newspaper headlines such as 'A CURRICULUM FOR BABIES' have been unhelpful. Clearly the document needs to be explored and discussed. Local authorities have the responsibility to deliver the programme, and nationally planning for training programmes are in the early stages.

What will this mean for you?

In the short term – very little! Early years and childcare teams from your local authorities will be likely to present a briefing to providers to broadly explain –

1. What the document (EYFS Pack) contains and what will be happening to existing training and future training programmes.

The document is made up of the following resources –

1. Statutory framework

2. Practice guidance

3. Principles into practice cards

4. Wall poster

5. CD-ROM.

You can obtain your own copy of the document, which contains all the resources, from the DfES publications line, 0845 6022260.

Alternatively, as your local authority may present you with your own copy, you may wish to just view it via www.teachernet.gov.uk/publications

What are the main sections of the document?

■ Learning and development requirements

■ Welfare Requirements.

How can this book help you?

The EYFS has a legal status through the Childcare Act 2006. From September 2008, it will be mandatory for all schools and early years providers in Ofsted registered settings attended by young children from birth to the end of the academic year in which a child has their fifth birthday.

The overarching aim of the EYFS is to help young children achieve the five outcomes of the Every Child Matters document by setting standards, providing for equality of opportunity, creating a framework for partnership working, improving quality and consistency, and laying a secure foundation for future learning. This book will explore the requirements to enable practitioners to deliver the EYFS in their own setting.

These are the welfare requirements –

1. Safeguarding and promoting children's welfare

2. Suitable people

3. Suitable premises, environment and equipment

4. Organisation

5. Documentation.

These are the learning and development requirements –

1. Personal, Social and Emotional development

2. Communication, Language and Literacy

3. Problem Solving, Reasoning and Numeracy

4. Knowledge and Understanding of the World

5. Physical Development

6. Creative Development.

What will be happening between May 2007 and September 2008?

Ofsted are carrying out a pilot programme between May-October 2007. Approximately one hundred providers nationally have been approached to be a part of the pilot programme of inspections of early years settings.

Why is this happening before September 2008?

Ofsted will be introducing a new inspection framework based on the requirements and supporting guidance of the EYFS to be used from September 2008. It is therefore necessary for a new inspection format to be tested out prior to September 2008. It is likely that the SEF (self evaluation form) being proposed will be used in the future. However, the SEF being used for the pilot scheme is subject to change. Ofsted are not in a position to finalise the SEF document at this time. The final evaluations of the pilot scheme will not happen before the end of 2007. Those currently involved in the pilot scheme include schools and early years settings, including childminders.

The inspection that will take place for those involved in the pilot scheme, will not count as a 'real' inspection. No reports will be published – however, should an inspector note any serious concerns about the quality of care during the visit, these concerns will be followed up.

Following a pilot inspection, the provider will receive verbal feedback and be sent a report. The report will be shared with parents, so that they too may comment on the new format and judgements made.

Following the evaluations of the pilot scheme, Ofsted will be able to decide about the actual documents for the EYFS inspections, which will include the SEF.

This book will explore the requirements of the EYFS –

1. What does this mean for your setting?

2. What do you need to do?

3. Good practice points.

The presentation of the document is what is 'new' – you will find that elements of the 14 National Standards of Care, the Birth – Three Framework, and the Curriculum Guidance for the Foundation Stage are still there, within the document.

Sources of information are: Primary Strategy, DfES and Ofsted. Sure Start websites and the Early Years Foundation Stage document/CD-ROM, Early Support.

Let's explore the pack!

What does the Early Years Foundation Stage document include?

As you open the resource pack, you will find a poster, principles into practice cards, a CD-ROM, and 2 booklets – the Statutory Framework and Practice Guidance.

The poster sets out –

1. Four overarching themes (headings)

2. Four principles (which summarise the underlying principles of the Birth – Three Framework, and the Curriculum Guidance for the Foundation Stage)

3. Sixteen commitments (what practitioners should be committed to doing – in other words, putting the principles into practice).

Once displayed, the poster will serve as a useful reminder of what the EYFS is all about – meeting the needs of children, and enabling each child to reach their potential.

You will find a total of 24 cards in the pack –

■ One card sets out the themes, principles and commitments

■ One card for each of the 16 commitments

■ One card for each of the 6 areas of learning

■ One card on child development exploring the overlapping ages and stages used within the EYFS.

All the cards together encompass all you have been familiar with in your work. When the EYFS was being produced, a full mapping exercise was carried out – time and attention was given to ensuring that the most of the statements relating to the birth – three framework and the curriculum guidance for the foundation stage were included.

So, you may wonder where the 14 National Standards of Care fit into all of this!

It is important to remember that the EYFS encompasses elements of the 14 National Standards of Care too. These Standards are now to be known as the Welfare Requirements. As the table below shows, the Welfare Requirements relate to the 5 outcomes, which we already know link to the National Standards. To support this, you will see on the bottom of the cards in the EYFS pack, which outcome relates to that particular card.

For example, if you look at

A Unique Child, card 1.1 which has Child Development as it's commitment, you will see along the bottom of that card, that MAKE A POSITIVE CONTRIBUTION is the associated outcome from Every Child Matters for this particular card. This applies to each of the cards. The information and guidance on each of the cards include what you need to consider for the Welfare Requirements which link to the outcome.

The principles of the EYFS are important, as they are intended to guide the work of all practitioners, and will form the basis of any training undertaken. Many settings will display the poster, as they did for the Birth – Three Framework. Understanding what the principles are all about is your starting point, so let's look at each one.

A Unique Child (theme)

Principle – Every child is a competent learner from birth who can be resilient, capable, confident and self-assured.

This principle is supported by 4 commitments, which describe how the principle can be put into practice:
- child development, inclusive practice,

Welfare Requirements	Relating to outcome	Links to elements of the Standards
Safeguarding and promoting children's welfare	Being healthy Staying safe Making a positive contribution	6,7,8,9,10,11,12,13
Suitable people	Staying safe	1
Suitable premises, environment and equipment	Staying safe	4,5
Organisation	Enjoy and achieve	2,3
Documentation	(Economic well being)	1-14

Table 1: Welfare Requirements and related outcomes linking to the National Standards

keeping safe and health and well-being.

Positive Relationships (theme)

Principle – Children learn to be strong and independent from a base of loving and secure relationships with parents and/or a key person.

This principle is supported by 4 commitments, which describe how the principle can be put into practice – respecting each other, parents as partners, supporting learning, and the key person.

Enabling Environments (theme)

Principle – The environment plays a key role in supporting and extending children's development and learning.

This principle is supported by 4 commitments, which describe how the principle can be put into practice - observation, assessment and planning, supporting every child, the learning environment and the wider context

Learning and Development (theme)

Principle – Children develop and learn in different ways and at different rates and all areas of learning and development are equally important and inter-connected.

This principle is supported by 4 commitments, which describe how the principle can be put into practice - play and exploration, active learning, creativity and critical thinking, and areas of learning and development.

As you consider the poster and the accompanying cards, you will find many links to the Birth – Three Framework and the Curriculum Guidance for the Foundation Stage, as well as the Welfare Requirements.

Let's look at one card as an example to understand the others –

Using the theme of A Unique Child, card 1.2 The commitment is Inclusive Practice. You will see that there are 3 boxes of statements that relate specifically to this card –

1. Equality and Diversity

2. Children's Entitlements

3. Early Support.

This is the front of the card – side 1. The bullet points under each of the three headings are the important aspects of the commitment for this particular card. At the bottom of the card, you will find the associated outcome that relates to Every Child Matters - Make a Positive Contribution.

Looking back to the table, you will see that the elements of the National Standards (and therefore the Welfare

A Unique Child *Every child is a competent learner from birth who can be resilient, capable, confident and self assured*	Positive Relationships *Children learn to be strong and independent from a base of loving and secure relationships with parents and/or a key person*	Enabling Environments *The environment plays a key role in supporting and extending children's development and learning*	Learning and Development *Children develop and learn in different ways and at different rates and all areas of learning and development are equally important and inter-connected*
1.1 Child Development – Child development A Skilful communicator A Competent Learner (Positive Contribution)	**2.1 Respecting Each Other –** Understanding feelings Friendships Professional relationships (Positive Contribution)	**3.1 Observation, Assessment and Planning –** Starting with the child Planning Assessment (Enjoy and Achieve)	**4.1 Play and Exploration –** Learning through experience Adult involvement Contexts for learning (Enjoy and Achieve)
1.2 Inclusive Practice – Equality and diversity Children's entitlements Early Support (Positive Contribution)	**2.2 Parents as Partners –** Respecting diversity Communication Learning Together (Positive Contribution)	**3.2 Supporting Every Child -** Children's needs The Learning journey Working together (Enjoy and Achieve)	**4.2 Active Learning –** Mental and physical involvement Decision making Personalised learning (Enjoy and Achieve)
1.3 Keeping Safe – Being safe and protected Discovering boundaries Making choices (Stay Safe)	**2.3 Supporting Learning –** Positive Interactions Listening to children Effective teaching (Positive Contribution)	**3.3 The Learning Environment -** The emotional environment The outdoor environment The indoor environment (Enjoy and Achieve)	**4.3 Creativity and Critical Thinking –** Making connections Transforming understanding Sustained shared thinking (Enjoy and Achieve)
1.4 Health and Well-being – Growing and developing Physical well-being Emotional well-being (Being Healthy)	**2.4 Key Person –** Secure attachment Shared Care Independence (Stay Safe)	**3.4 The Wider Context -** Transitions and continuity Multi-agency working The community (Positive Contribution)	**4.4 Six Areas of Learning and Development –** (Enjoy and Achieve)

Table 2: The principles of the EYFS

Requirements) that broadly link to this particular commitment are Standards 6,7,8,9,10,11,12,13. The Welfare Requirement is Safeguarding and promoting children's welfare.

If you turn the card over, you will see a reminder at the top about which theme and commitment this card relates to. The information on this side of the card is all about putting the principle into practice. There are three boxes to consider.

1. Effective practice

2. Challenges and dilemmas

3. Reflecting on practice.

All of the 16 commitment cards follow the same format for side 2 of the cards. Side one will differ for each card, as it is specific in describing that particular commitment. The questions on the cards under the heading of 'Reflecting on practice' bring together the relevant parts from the Birth –Three Framework, the Curriculum Guidance for the Foundation Stage, and the Welfare Requirements.

On the bottom of side 2 of the card, you will see a reference to KEEP (Key Elements of Effective Practice). This is a very useful document that you should become familiar with. Key Elements of Effective Practice requires practitioners to reflect and use their

own learning to improve their work with young children and their families in ways which are sensitive, positive and non-judgemental. For example in card 1.2 (Inclusive Practice) you will see that the KEEP statement is 'Practice in meeting all children's needs, learning styles and interests'.

While exploring the pack, practitioners may recognise for themselves that they may need further training in, for example, improving their relationships with children and adults, or their understanding of the complexities of the ways in which children learn and develop. KEEP is a useful tool to enable practitioners to consider their knowledge, skills and understanding, and to think about how they may improve in the following ways –

■ Relationships with both children and adults

■ Understanding of the individual and diverse ways that children develop and learn

■ Knowledge and understanding in order to actively support and extend children's learning in and across all areas and aspects of learning

■ Practice in meeting all children's needs, learning styles and interests

■ Work with parents, carers and the wider community

■ Work with other professionals within and beyond the setting.

The message is that 'each of the 6 areas are 'key' to effective practice and each is an 'element' in its own right. Each is dependent on all the others and each contributes to the whole'.

EPPE (Effective Provision of Pre-School Education)

In considering best practice, many practitioners have referred to the EPPE final report (2004) which gave details of a major study of a national sample of young children's development (intellectual and social/behavioural) between the ages of 3 and 7 years. To investigate the effects of pre-school education for 3 and 4 year olds, the EPPE team collected a wide range of information on over 3000 children, their parents, their home environments and the pre-schools they attended. This is important, because one of the main aims of the EYFS is to improve the quality of early years practice. EPPE research has shown that better quality early years settings means better social and cognitive outcomes for children which will last well into Key Stage 1 and Key Stage 2. Good early years practice therefore means more children meeting the Every Child Matters outcomes.

There are two booklets in your pack -

1. The Statutory Framework for the Early Years Foundation Stage, which sets out the legal requirements and statutory guidance for all settings. The booklet heading of 'framework' may be misleading to some – in fact, this booklet states what you MUST do, not to just be considered. Much of the training provided by your local authority will focus on your legal responsibilities

2. The Practice Guidance for the Early Years Foundation Stage, which is more than 'guidance'. In addition to the legal requirements, this book contains additional advice as well as the detail of the areas of learning and development, including the EYFS Profile.

The CD-ROM has in depth information on the EYFS that is likely to be used in training, as video material is available. It is from here that you may access the information on effective practice, research findings, Early Support materials, and many other links to websites for your information.

You can obtain your own copies of these related documents through the DfES website (publications) or by calling 0845 6022260.

The Principles into Practice cards are colour coded, and introduce you to an overview of child development. As we know, the EYFS covers the 0-5 years age group. For a greater understanding of child development, the EYFS has the breakdown of ages as follows – you will notice that there is an overlap of the age groups –

■ Birth – 11 months

■ 8 months – 20 months

■ 16 months – 26 months

■ 22 months – 36 months

■ 30 months – 50 months

■ 40 months – 60 months +.

Many people will look at this, and may conclude that for most people, after 2 years of age, children usually have their ages stated as, for example, two and a half, or just three years old. You may consider using the ages as shown above or you may present the ages as –

■ Birth – 11 months

■ 8 months – 1 year 8 months

■ 1 year 4 months – 2 years 2 months

■ 1 year 10 months – 3 years

■ 2 years 6 months – 4 years 2 months

■ 3 years 4 months – 5 years +.

The overlap allows for stages of development within an age range from birth – five years.

Your knowledge of child development is crucial. The broad ages of development within the EYFS is your starting point.

All children are different and to reflect this, age ranges have been overlapped in the EYFS to create broad developmental phases. This emphasises that each child's progress is individual to them and that different children develop at different rates. A child does not suddenly move from one phase to another, and they do not make progress in all areas at the same time. However, there are some important 'steps' for each child to take along their own developmental

pathway. These are shown on the areas of Learning and Development in the sections 'Look, listen and note', and 'Development matters'. There are six broad developmental phases.

If you refer to the card 'Child Development Overview' within your pack, you will find the six broad developmental phases. This information will be of use to the practitioner, as they begin to more fully appreciate the need to understand what to expect within the age ranges. You may consider the benefits of displaying this card alongside the poster in your setting.

The Early Years Foundation Stage

What are the requirements?

These come under 2 headings –

Learning and Development requirements

These cover:

1. The Early Learning Goals

2. The Educational Programmes

3. The Assessment Arrangements.

Welfare Requirements

These cover:

1. Safeguarding and promoting children's welfare

2. Suitable people

3. Suitable premises, environment and equipment

4. Organisation

5. Documentation.

Ofsted will carry out inspections from September 2008, to ensure that registered settings are meeting the requirements of the EYFS. It is likely that the inspectors will take into account the information from the SEF (self evaluation form) that you will have completed in readiness for your inspection. Remember that it is likely that the SEF being proposed will be used in the future. However, the SEF being used for the pilot scheme is subject to change. Ofsted are not in a position to finalise the SEF document at this time.

The SEF is likely to be presented in 2 parts –

Part A: Evaluation

Section 1: Outcomes for children

1(a): How well do children enjoy and achieve in your setting?

1(b): How do you ensure the well-being of each child in your setting?

2: How well do children learn to stay safe?

3: How well do children learn to be healthy?

4: How well do children learn to make a positive contribution?

5 How well do children develop skills for the future?

Section 2: What you do to promote the outcomes

6: How effective are you in helping children to learn and develop?

7: How effective is the welfare of the children in the EYFS promoted?

Section 3: Leadership and Management

8: How effectively is your provision led and managed?

Section 4: Improving your setting

9(a): What improvements have been made to the provision since the last inspection?

9(b): What are your plans for future improvement?

Section 5: Overall effectiveness

10: Overall, how effective and inclusive is your provision in meeting the needs of children who attend?

Part B: Factual information about your setting

This section covers the location and history of your setting, your registration details, how many staff are employed and some details relating to qualifications of staff. So, we broadly need to consider the 10 questions within the 5 sections of part A.

■ What does this mean for your setting?

■ What do you need to do?

■ Effective practice.

For each of the sections within your self-evaluation form you will assess yourselves as –

■ Outstanding (excellent)

■ Good (strong)

■ Satisfactory (could do better)

■ Inadequate (not good enough).

Let's look at Part A: Evaluation

Outcomes for children

We need to consider how well children learn and develop in your setting in relation to their starting points and capabilities, the extent to which children are active learners, are creative and are able to think in a critical sense. We need to consider whether each child's progress is consistently better than any other child or falls below the progress of other children. Crucially, we also need to consider children's enjoyment of, and attitudes towards learning, and how they are given opportunities to work independently.

We need to consider how you can encourage children to behave in ways that are safe for themselves and other people in the setting, and how you show the level of the children's understanding of dangers and how they may stay safe.

We need to consider the extent to which you setting helps children understand and adopt healthy habits, and the extent to which children make healthy choices about what they eat and drink.

We need to consider how you encourage children to join in, make friends and feel part of the setting, and for each child, the extent to which children respond to the expectations of those who work with them. We need to consider ways in which you encourage children to make choices and decisions.

If children are to develop skills for the future, we need to give thought to the ways in which the children show progress in communicating, levels of literacy, numeracy and ICT (information and communication technology).

We need to consider ways in which you encourage all children to become active, inquisitive and independent learners, develop their skills in being a part of a social group, and how they solve problems. We need to think about how you give the children a greater understanding of the wider world through their play.

Of course, what every practitioner does to promote the outcomes is important.

Remember that the Every Child Matters outcomes are what you are already working towards – the EYFS is not 'new'. It brings together the Birth – Three Framework, the Curriculum Guidance for Foundation Stage, and elements of the 14 National Standards of Care. Most of the things we are giving consideration to now, are likely to have been addressed already in your setting – what is new is the presentation of the EYFS, and the way in which you complete the self-evaluation form to bring your practice into line with the EYFS.

We need to think about how effective you are in helping children to learn and develop – how you support each child's learning, and how you can create a learning environment which will help children progress towards the early learning goals. This may an area of development for you and/or your colleagues. Training for all practitioners in how to observe, assess and plan for purposeful play and exploration, is available though your local authority. Practitioners may need guidance on ways in which to balance adult led and child initiated activities.

The Welfare Requirements give you the opportunity to think about 5 areas.

Consider how well you –

■ safeguard and promote the welfare of each child

■ ensure the health and well-being of each child

■ guide/teach children about keeping safe

■ encourage children to develop appropriate habits and behaviour

■ ensure the suitability and qualifications of people who are responsible for the children, and for those who have access to the children

■ ensure the suitability of the indoor and outside environments.

Policies and procedures are required for all group settings. It is disappointing to many that childminders will not be expected to produce key written policies and procedures, as these documents safeguard the practices of the practitioner, whether they work alone or within a group setting. It could be agued that a childminder who does produce written policies and procedures, has given more regard to their service than a childminder who has not done so. An inspector may judge that the first childminder as outstanding due to the extra written evidence produced. This would seem unfair to the second childminder, who has not been expected to produce such paperwork. It may be recommended within your local authority that, for good practice, if nothing else, policies and procedures should be in place for ALL settings, including childminders. Quality improvement schemes, such as the NCMA Children Come First, are likely to continue to ask for written policies and procedures.

Other considerations for showing how effective you are in leading and managing your setting centre are related to risk assessments, links with parents and carers, and broadly how you have integrated the care and education within EYFS. This will possibly link to you producing evidence on how you are considering making improvements within your setting.

Finally, you will reach a conclusion about how effective you think you are in terms of meeting the individual care and learning needs of the children in your setting.

What does this mean for your setting?

The requirements of the EYFS have statutory force by virtue of Section 44 (1) of the Childcare Act 2006.

The Learning and Development requirements are given legal force by the EYFS Order 2007, made under Section 39 (1) (a) of the Childcare Act 2006.

The Welfare Requirements are given legal force by Regulations made under Section 39 (1) (b) of the Childcare Act 2006.

Together, the Order, the Regulations and the Statutory Framework document make up the legal basis of the EYFS.

This means that every registered setting has a duty to ensure that their provision complies with all of the requirements, as well as taking into account the statutory guidance. It is widely accepted that requirements must be met – all settings have been used to meeting requirements – the things you must do. However, the word 'guidance' implies that you only need to consider certain things.

We must be clear that –

All providers MUST have regard to the guidance, which means they MUST take it into account, and if they decide to depart from it, they MUST have clear reasons for doing so and be able to demonstrate that their alternative approach achieves the ends described in the guidance.

Ofsted will take account of any failure to have regard to the guidance when exercising its functions, including any proceedings which are brought under the Act.

It is therefore important as we look at ways in which the EYFS can be delivered, that the requirements and guidance are given equal regard.

What do you need to do?

Introduce the document to practitioners who work in your setting – this will be an opportunity for everyone to appreciate that the work they do already is within the EYFS. Use the poster as your starting point so that everyone is clear about the four themes:

■ A Unique Child

■ Positive Relationships

■ Enabling Environments

■ Learning and Development.

THE PRINCIPLES, which support effective practice

1. Every child is a competent learner from birth who can be resilient, capable, confident and self-assured

2. Children learn to be strong and independent from a base of loving and secure relationships with parents and/or a key person

3. The environment plays a key role in supporting and extending children's development and learning

4. Children learn and develop in different ways and at different rates and all areas of learning and development are equally important and inter-connected.

THE 16 COMMITMENTS, which describe how the Principle can be put into practice.

THE ASPECTS, which support the commitments.

The poster clearly shows all of this.

Everyone working within the EYFS needs to remember that:

Children learn best when they are healthy, safe and secure, when their individual needs are met and when they have positive relationships with the adults caring for them.

Each of the cards in your pack provides you with information about effective practice across the **THEMES** of the EYFS. The requirements are put into context within the cards, describing the ways in which practitioners should support the development, learning and care of the babies and young children.

It is worth looking at the prompts and questions on the cards to establish where training may be needed for staff. How can you do this?

Allow staff time to look at the cards, to explore the **PRINCIPLES**.

Ask the staff to look at the questions, and decide where they feel they may need further training.

Let's use **four** cards as examples –

■ Card – A Unique Child 1.3 Keeping Safe.

■ Card - Positive Relationships 2.4 Key Person

■ Card - Enabling Environments 3.1 Observation, Assessment and Planning

■ Card - Learning and Development 4.1 Play and Exploration

A Unique Child 1.3 Keeping Safe

Look at the headings on side one of the card –

■ Being safe and protected

■ Discovering boundaries

■ Making choices.

These headings are specific to this card. The commitment (statement) that applies to the card is clearly shown at the top –

Young children are **vulnerable**. They develop **resilience** when the **physical** and **psychological well-being is protected** by adults.

Why are some of the words printed in bold?

These are the key words that apply to this card. If you look on the other cards, you will see that they also have bold print to identify the key words for those cards.

So, let's focus on **vulnerable, resilience, physical** and **psychological well-being**

Babies and young children have little sense of danger – they can only learn how to assess the risks they may face with the guidance from adults. Young children need to know the limits and boundaries on what they may or may not do for their own safety and for the safety of all. Practitioners need to guard against making choices for the children – easier said than done!

So, how can the practitioner make use of this card?

1. Reading the statements on side one of the card, and reflecting on how they, as individuals, support the babies and young children to feel safe and protected, whilst allowing for choices to be made

2. Looking at the questions on side two of the card – can the practitioner answer the questions, based on the

effective practice shown in the top box?

The Challenges and Dilemmas are useful for training purposes – it may be that these could be used as a focus for discussion in your staff meetings. Childminders on a Network could explore these challenges as they meet for support with their Co-ordinator and Early Years teachers. Registered childminders who are not on a Network may attend training, which is open to all early years and childcare providers, to discuss ways in which the challenges may be addressed in their own homes.

At the bottom of the card on side one, you will see reference to Every Child Matters, and the outcome that applies to this card. This is Stay Safe. Therefore you will see that the Welfare Requirements linked to this card are included by reference to the outcome.

At the bottom of the card on side two, you will see reference to KEEP, and the statement from KEEP that applies to this card. It is 'Relationships with both children and adults'. You can order your own copy of the KEEP document from the DfES publications department (telephone) 0845 6022260. Reference number 1201-2005 G

By accessing the CD-ROM, you will find the section on Effective Practice - Keeping Safe.

The section covers –

Key Messages

■ Actively listen to and observe children

■ Be vigilant

■ Constantly assess risks

■ Share concerns

■ Keep the setting clean, safe and secure

■ Update training regularly

■ Maintain relevant documentation

■ Ensure premises, equipment and materials are appropriate for the children attending the setting

■ Foster children's curiosity, drives and adventurous spirits; help them to recognise boundaries; teach them how to make choices, assess risks, and keep themselves safe.

The central aim of Every Child Matters is to improve outcomes for every child and to narrow the gap between those who thrive and those who do not. Ofsted (2005) 'staying safe' relates to ensuring that children have security, stability and care, and that they are protected from accidental injury, discrimination, all forms of abuse and neglect, bullying and anti-social behaviour'.

Effective practice

'Keeping safe is an important principle, not simply because the law requires it, but because young children are vulnerable, being relatively small and physically weak, dependent on others for their needs and for their protection. When we take on the care of a child, we are accountable for that child's safety and healthy development. Human life is fragile but it is also an adventure and so, while maintaining continuous risk assessment, practitioners must remember children's natural curiosity and their drive to explore, to learn about their world and to test themselves and their abilities'.

Refer back to the card 1.3 and the headings on side one –

■ **Being safe and protected**

■ **Discovering boundaries**

■ **Making choices.**

Effective practice for these headings include –

1. Being safe and protected

The importance of your partnership with parents – essential if both parents and children are to feel safe and welcome to the setting. Parents will feel more confident about a setting that shares policies and procedures about how the children will be kept safe. It is important to reassure parents that policies are acted on in practice, and that staff regularly update their training on safety. You must keep written records of any existing injuries and injuries that occur whilst the child is in your care. These reports must show how any injury was dealt with and any other action necessary. Parents should be encouraged to contribute to their child's records, particularly where information is shared about their child's emotional well-being and contentment within the setting. You should be sharing information about the child's development and interests, and, importantly, when a child shows anxiety or stress.

If you manage a setting consider the following –

a) How do you deploy staff to ensure that all children are well supervised?

b) How do you ensure that all adults are aware of their responsibilities and are abler to manage risk assessment and children's risk-taking effectively?

c) How do you ensure the safety of the children and premises at all times?

d) How do you ensure, in group settings, that the designated person for Health and Safety knows about relevant legislation, and how to record risk assessments?

e) How do you ensure, in group settings, that the designated person for safeguarding and protecting children has attended relevant training to know how they deal with concerns promptly, appropriately and sensitively? Have you thought about issues of confidentiality?

f) How do you ensure that unsuitable adults do not gain access to children in the setting?

g) How certain are you that all staff are clear about who is authorised to collect individual children? What systems do you have in place for this?

h) How do you ensure that all staff have knowledge of individual children's medical conditions, so that any necessary action is ensured?

i) Do you gain parents' written consent to take children on outings, and ensure that necessary systems are in place for the needs of the children when they are taken off site?

The Childcare Act requires that records are kept with details about each child, together with information about the premises and every practitioner.

If you are a practitioner, consider the following –

■ Do you minimise risk at all times by ongoing risk assessment?

■ Do you know where the appropriate fire equipment is sited, and know your responsibilities in the event of an emergency, such as a fire?

■ Do you report hazards?

■ Do you check entrances and exits so that children cannot leave the premises, and that unknown people cannot enter?

■ Have you up to date health and safety and child protection knowledge?

■ Do you ensure that babies and young children are able to sleep safely, and do you check them regularly?

■ Do you know how you may assist children to make choices and begin to understand risk?

■ Are you confident in promoting the children's ability to deal with unwanted touch as they get older and to feel secure about talking to trusting adults?

■ Do you know about all the children's medical needs and your responsibilities in administering medication?

■ Do you ensure that the indoor and outside environments are effectively organised for safety and the children's enjoyment?

■ Are you aware of the appropriate adult: child ratios?

2. Discovering boundaries

This is not about just about the 'rules' of your setting. It is important for children to know what is acceptable and what is not acceptable in terms of behaviour. One aspect of young children's learning that is crucial during the EYFS is that of respect for others, focusing on how we treat others, and how we keep each other safe.

Your partnership with parents is important so that children have consistent messages about how to behave in acceptable ways, and what may happen in terms of safety or well-being, if unacceptable behaviours occur.

3. Making choices

How do you create a child-friendly environment where children can explore and take 'safe' risks while being appropriately supervised, so that, once mobile, children can move freely and address challenges for themselves? This is something that needs careful consideration, as you need to think about the interests of the individual child, each child's capabilities, and how you meet each child's needs. If you allow babies and young children to follow their own lines of enquiry – in other words, what they want to do/explore, they will gain confidence in their own abilities to challenge themselves. Children do not always have to be in sight – if the environment is safe, what happens within the environment can allow for independent choice and 'out of sight' play opportunities. The home corner is an example of this type of play.

Your knowledge of child development is very important within the EYFS. Under 'Keeping Safe', you need to think about the following –

Babies and young children rely on trusted adults to keep them safe.

Children do not recognise that harm may come to them from for example, water, or the speed of a moving vehicle.

Young children are competent learners so we can help them acquire skills which will eventually help them keep themselves safe in such situations.

So, what development points do you need to consider for Keeping Safe?

Let's refer back to, and use, the age groups within the EYFS.

Between birth – 11 months

Babies and young children have no sense of danger; they learn about dangerous situations by looking at the faces of and reactions of the people they know and trust. While some babies have begun to stand and walk within this phase, most that are mobile will be rolling or crawling. They will usually gain control of their eyes, necks and hands in this first year and they will be able to express their desires through increasingly defined signs and vocalisations. Dangers become increasingly possible as babies explore their environment through touch and taste, as well as smell, sight and hearing.

8 months – 20 months (8 months – 1 year 8 months)

Even in this age group, babies and young children have no sense of

danger. They are likely to have become very mobile during this phase and will be beginning to assert their own wills.

16 months – 26 months (1 year 4 months – 2 years 2 months)

It is usually during this phase that children's awareness of other minds and the reconfiguring of their brains takes place. They are likely to have begun to use language to express themselves and influence others and they are working out what makes the familiar people in their lives 'tick'. They may test boundaries and attempt physical feats that defy their carer's advice, as part of their growing independence.

22 months – 36 months (1 year 10 months – 3 years)

Children's imaginations will have become much more vivid by now. They learn about dangerous situations from stories and will have some fears that will manifest themselves in play and in nightmares. Others may need protection from trying out exploits seen on television and in films. At the same time, practitioners and parents are faced with the increasingly difficult task of helping children to understand the dangers in the world and to assess risk, while at the same time reassuring rather than alarming them.

30 months – 50 months (2 years 6 months – 4 years 2 months)

Each successive phase builds on and incorporates preceding phases, but it must be remembered that children will sometimes regress and behave as they did when younger, especially when they are tired or upset. So it is important to maintain vigilance, even as children seem more capable and knowledgeable. During this phase other children who are their friends will have become part of the group of familiar people who are central to their happiness. They will become more secure emotionally if those friends move on to primary school with them after this phase.

40 months – 60 months (3 years 4 months – 5 years +)

During this phase children will have become adept at both gross and fine motor control. They may need reminding about climbing, riding and balancing, safety, and the safety of others. They will be skilled tool users, and yet will need to be reminded about safe use of hammers, saws, knives, ropes and other potentially dangerous materials. Adult:child ratios at this stage mean that children in this phase need to be supported in taking a little more responsibility for themselves and building on earlier teaching about risk assessment. They will need help from their parents, friends and their new teachers and teaching assistants to cope emotionally in the larger context of the primary school. Practitioners will need to assess risk in their own setting, for example, whether the children in the reception year would benefit from a separate play area from the rest of the school, or whether mixing with older children, indoors or outside, will not only be safe, but have positive effects on their learning.

So, how does 'Keeping Safe' relate to the specific areas of Learning and Development?

We have six areas to consider –

Personal, Social and Emotional development

Having someone to whom they are special, who cares for, respects, provides emotional support for and loves them, and who provides safety and security, is essential for young children's development. Being acknowledged and affirmed by important people in their lives leads to secure attachments and to children gaining confidence and inner strength. They will want to explore, physically, socially and emotionally, and become as independent as possible. Observing children and planning how to enable this for all children is an important adult responsibility. Positive role models among the adults and other children with whom they share their lives help them to be resilient, capable, sociable and strong. Through these relationships and modelling, they will learn to love and care for themselves and other people as family and friends, and to love and to care for the world they live in.

Communication, Language and Literacy

Actively listening to babies and young children encourages them to express themselves, to voice their desires and fears, likes and dislikes. Attentive conversations with babies and young children that involve treating them as if they understand what is being said, even before they know the language being used, together with the relevant facial and bodily expressions to assist the flow of meaning, help them develop their communication and social skills. This acts as model for their later interactions with both adults and children. Children are keen to know what is meant by print they see around them and this will include safety notices they see in your setting and in the world at large. Sometimes children will write their own warning notices during play activities.

Problem Solving, Reasoning and Numeracy

Problem solving skills are developed when young children need to carry out risk assessments. They will assiduously help with counting children when on outings and so on and will discuss topics such as how high a tower of bricks can be before it becomes a safety hazard.

Knowledge and Understanding of the World

Children acquire a range of skills, knowledge and attitudes related to knowledge and understanding of the world in many ways. As babies they acutely observe their surroundings and the people who inhabit their world and how these people behave; they learn that by exploring their world through their senses. Young children learn by acting as if they are asking the question 'What does this do?' and having carried out some exploration, 'What can I do with this?' The objects and events they explore will include other people, the environment, creatures, materials, toys and equipment. Children therefore need settings in which they can play and explore safely and where they are encouraged to predict possible outcomes of their own actions, as in risk assessments.

Physical Development

Physical development may be seen as the most important in relation to Keeping Safe, and clearly children's physical safety and protection from physical harm is a major responsibility for practitioners. It is also one where risk assessments by adults, and in time with the children themselves, are crucial, because young children need to be active, to use space and equipment in progressively challenging ways, in order to gain confidence, learn and develop.

Creative Development

Using and adapting stories, music and dance, talking with children about their drawings and paintings, and

observing children's dramatic play are all important aspects of Keeping Safe. They can be used to enhance children's feelings of competence, confidence and strength. During the creative process, children often express and reveal their fears and concerns, and adults should be alert to any anxieties displayed. They should act appropriately by listening to children, talking with colleagues and parents and taking supportive action to dispel any concerns the child may have. In some cases, simply reassuring a child may well be enough to make them feel comfortable. There is, however, some evidence that in relaxing situations that are not obviously connected with on-going events, issues about the way a child may have treated may be revealed and lead to concerns of child abuse. Such concerns must always be taken seriously and addressed appropriately. Adults should be trained in responding sensitively to any concerns expressed verbally or non-verbally by any child.

The theme of A Unique Child has 4 commitments. We have considered Keeping Safe in detail. The other 3 commitments are –

Child Development

Babies and children develop individual ways and at varying rates. Every area of development – physical, cognitive, linguistic, spiritual, social and emotional – is equally important.

Key Messages for Child Development are:

■ Every child is a unique individual whose development usually follows predictable patterns

■ Rates of development vary from child to child and from time to time

■ Many factors affect a child's development, for example, low birth weight, a recent move or their family being under stress

■ Each child's personal story is important and is the starting point for supporting their development and learning

■ Where there are concerns about a child's development always talk to parents and seek help from other professionals.

Inclusive Practice

The diversity of individuals and communities is valued and respected. No child or family is discriminated against.

Key Messages for Inclusive Practice are:

■ Inclusion is about attitudes as well as behaviour and practices

■ The attitudes of young children towards diversity are affected by the behaviour of adults around them and by whether all children and families using the setting are valued and welcomed

■ The principle of individualised learning underpinning the EYFS extends to all children; early years practitioners have a responsibility to promote the development of all children within the EYFS

■ Working in partnership with families is particularly important when a child had additional support needs. Joint planning that involved parents and carers and two way exchange of information about a child is critical to success

■ Careful tracking of development by settings and parents working together supports earlier discussion and response to emerging special educational needs

■ Focused discussion and training is needed to help practitioners and settings consider the nature of discrimination and develop inclusive practice

■ Inclusion is not optional; children have defined entitlements in this area and settings have legal responsibilities.

Health and Well–Being.

Children's health is an integral part of their emotional, mental, social, environmental and spiritual well-being and is supported by attention to these aspects – growing and developing, physical well-being and emotional well-being.

Key Messages for Health and Well-Being are:

■ Resilience is promoted through attachment and each child being special to at least one significant person

■ Children's dietary and physical needs underpin their ability to develop

■ Opportunities to explore and play in a safe and secure environment, and children's mobility and movement, are important for their development

■ Brain development depends on nourishment; a good diet, in both the form of good food and of physical and psychological stimulation

■ Reasonable rules, which fit with children's rhythms and give a pattern to life, matter

■ Parents, as well as children, matter

■ Young children enjoy contributing to life in their setting and being with their friends

■ Child abuse, neglect and failure to thrive impact on children's health and well-being

■ Babies and young children with special needs have additional requirements. They need access to similar experiences and opportunities as other children, in both a philosophical as well as practical sense

■ It is important that each child knows their key person

■ Senior practitioners in your setting should be designated and trained to be responsible for child protection issues and health and safety

■ Communities and the public need help to understand the importance of positive interactions and experiences in the first five years of life, for all areas of development and for enjoyment

■ Strong links between the setting and other professionals such as health visitors and community paediatricians are vital.

Positive Relationships 2.4
Key Person

Look at the headings on side one of the card –

■ Secure attachment

■ Shared care

■ Independence.

These headings are specific to this card. The commitment (statement) that applies to the card is clearly shown at the top –

A key person has **special responsibilities** for working with a small number of children, giving them the reassurance to feel safe and cared for and building relationships with their parents.

Why are some of the words printed in bold?

These are the key words that apply to this card. If you look on the other cards, you will see that they also have bold print to identify the key words for those cards.

So, let's focus on **special relationships** and **safe**

A key person develops a genuine bond with children and offers a settled, close relationship. This close relationship does not undermine the children's relationships with their parents. Babies and young children become independent when they feel safe, when they are able to depend on key people for reassurance and comfort.

So, how can the practitioner make use of this card?

1. Reading the statements on side one of the card, and reflecting on how they as individuals support babies and young children in forming close, emotional relationships

2. Looking at the questions on side two of the card – can the practitioner answer the questions, based on the effective practice shown in the top box?

The Challenges and Dilemmas are useful for training purposes – it may be that these could be used as a focus for discussion in your staff meetings. Childminders on a Network could explore these challenges as they meet for support with their Co-ordinator and Early Years teachers. Registered childminders who are not on a Network may attend training, which is open to all early years and childcare providers, to discuss ways in which the challenges may be addressed in their own homes.

At the bottom of the card on side one, you will see reference to Every Child Matters, and the outcome that applies to this card. It is Stay Safe. Therefore you will see that the welfare requirements linked to this card are included by reference to the outcome.

At the bottom of the card on side two, you will see reference to KEEP, and the statement from KEEP that applies to this card. It is Relationships with both children and adults. You can order your own copy of the KEEP document from the DfES publications department (telephone) 0845 6022260 Reference 2101-2005 G.

By accessing the CD-ROM, you will find the section on Effective Practice – Keeping Safe.

The section covers –

Key Messages

■ Being clear about why the key person commitment is so important, and why working in this way is so important to children

■ Planning for effective practice including head teachers and managers finding time to support

practitioners by listening regularly and carefully to their experiences

■ Being prepared to take time to develop the key person approach.

The central aim of Every Child Matters is to improve outcomes for every child and to narrow the gap between those who thrive and those who do not. Ofsted says 'staying safe' relates to 'ensuring that children have security, stability and care, and that they are protected from accidental injury, discrimination, all forms of abuse and neglect, bullying and anti-social behaviour'.

Effective practice

'Keeping safe is an important principle, not simply because the law requires it, but because young children are vulnerable, being relatively small and physically weak, dependent on others for their needs and for their protection. When we take on the care of a child, we are accountable for that child's safety and healthy development. Human life is fragile but it is also an adventure and so, while maintaining continuous risk assessment, practitioners must remember children's natural curiosity and their drive to explore, to learn about their world and to test themselves and their abilities'.

Refer back to the card 2.4 and the headings on side one –

■ Secure attachment

■ Shared care

■ Independence.

We need to consider some issues for the practitioner in relation to these headings –

What are the benefits for the parents, key person and the child?

The benefits for parents are firstly, peace of mind – they know that someone in the setting has a particular close relationship with their child, and will meet their child's needs. For parents to have relationship with someone who can share the pleasures (and stresses) of child rearing is important they know they can liaise with the key person who loves their baby or child too. Being a key person is not always easy – the role involves hard work, and a big professional and

emotional commitment. This does not come naturally to everyone. However, by gaining experience of working closely with families, practitioners will begin to appreciate the importance of the role - the impact they are likely to have on a child's well-being, their mental health, and their opportunities to think and learn.

Practitioners will realise the benefits that the key person role has within the setting – they are likely to feel more satisfied in their work, and will therefore provide better care and learning for the children.

For a baby or young child to know that there is a special person to care for them while they are away from home is reassuring.

Why is the key person important?

The quality of care young children receive makes a big difference to each child, day by day, and for their future. The key person has a responsibility to bring this quality into a child's life while they are away from home – this can be enormously demanding for the practitioner, in emotional terms. By remaining attentive and affectionate, the key person will ensure that the relationship with the baby or young child will develop to benefit the child and the practitioner.

Challenges and Dilemmas

The most obvious question is 'how close is too close?' This is a dilemma for some people, as they are concerned that children may become too dependent on them. Attachment issues, such as a parent feeling that their child is 'closer' to the practitioner than to themselves need to be addressed. Parents need to be reassured that their children are being supported and cared for as individuals. The role of the key person in the setting is to provide this reassurance to parents.

If you are a practitioner, discuss your responsibilities with the parents of the children –

1. Your role is to help the baby or child to become familiar with the setting and to feel confident and safe within it.

2. Your role is to develop a genuine bond with the children and to offer a close relationship

3. Your role is to encourage the child to feel happy and secure, to be confident to explore and try out new things.

Your relationship with parents is crucial – you need to be 'close' to the parents too, to get to know the family well, in the child's best interests. Remember at all times that you should be developing a professional relationship with the families, which is not the same as developing a friendship. It is very important to think about the feelings and points of view of practitioners as well as the feelings and points of view of parents and their children. No practitioner should ever feel alone in their work with families – for example, support would be needed if a parent approached the key person to discuss a family situation. An unexpected death, divorce or separation, as examples, would mean that the key person may need to refer to others for ways in which the family may receive appropriate support. It is important for managers to allow time for practitioners to seek advice.

'The key person has the opportunity and time to develop attachments between individual children, individual practitioners and family units -close relationships that are establishing young children's emotional security and self-esteem. Children must come first and a key persons approach of continuity, health and learning

for children and their families should become a reality and not just the exception for a few'

The theme of Positive Relationships has 4 commitments. We have considered Key Person in detail. The other 3 commitments are –

Respecting Each Other

Every interaction is based on caring professional relationships and respectful acknowledgement of the feelings of children and their families.

Key Messages for Respecting Each Other are:

■ Respect for others is the basis of good relationships

■ Babies and children learn who they are and what they can accomplish through relationships

■ Children learn about others through their relationships. They become aware that others may have different needs, feelings and ideas from their own

■ Through friendships, children learn that there are different viewpoints than their own and develop interpersonal skills

■ Effective relationships foster children's emotional and social development

■ Within secure relationships, children feel safe to express feelings and learn to cope with and understand them

■ Responsive, supportive, warm and respectful relationships between children are bolstered when these qualities feature in interactions between adults

■ Good relationships between practitioners and parents enable practitioners to build on family and cultural practices when tuning in to children's needs and ideas.

Parents as Partners

Parents are children's first and most enduring educators. When parents and practitioners work together in early years settings, the results have a positive impact on children's development and learning.

Key Messages for Parents as Partners are:

■ Parents provide a learning environment, which is enduring and comprehensive. It begins even before birth, operates beyond the child's day at the setting and provides continuity as the child transfers from one setting to another

■ Over 70% of children's lives are spent, not in a setting, but with their family and the wider community. Therefore home and community must be recognised as significant learning environments in the lives of children

■ All parents can enhance their child's development and learning

■ Parents have the right to play a central role in making decisions about their child's care and education at every level

■ Successful relationships between parents and educators can have long-lasting and beneficial effects on children's learning and well-being

■ Successful relationships become partnerships when ther is two-way communication and parents and practitioners really listen to each other and value each other's views and support in achieving the best outcomes for each child.

Supporting Learning

Warm, trusting relationships with knowledgeable adults support children's learning more effectively than any amount of resources.

Key Messages for Supporting Learning are:

■ Observing, enabling and facilitating are the key ingredients of teaching in the EYFS

■ The term 'support' includes the care, attentiveness and interaction that facilitate learning, with teaching belonging within this

■ Bringing together knowledge about individual children and knowledge about what they can learn, enables practitioners to plan and provide for meaningful next steps in learning

■ Adult support in the EYFS must include scope for independent learning, timely guidance and

on-going reassurance and encouragement to enable young children to feel secure, valued and individually well care for. There should be a balance of child initiated and adult initiated activities

■ Children learn best through their interactions with people who know and relate to them well

■ Practitioners should place great store on listening to what parents say about their children's needs and how they make themselves understood

■ Listening to children enables practitioners to create meaningful activities that help them to make connections and tackle new ideas

■ When children get to know practitioners, they trust and rely on them to support, encourage and 'feed' their investigations

■ Through play, in which they take the lead and make choices, children develop their own thinking and encounter new ideas.

Enabling Environments 3.1 Observation, Planning and Assessment

Look at the headings on side one of the card –

■ Starting with the child

■ Planning

■ Assessment.

These headings are specific to this card. The commitment (statement) that applies to the card is clearly shown at the top –

Babies and young children are **individuals first, each with a unique profile of abilities**. Schedules and routines should flow with the child's needs. All planning starts with observing children in order to understand and consider their current interests, development and learning.

Why are some of the words printed in bold?

These are the key words that apply to this card. If you look on the other cards, you will see that they also have bold print to identify the key words for those cards.

So, let's focus on **individual first, each with a unique profile of abilities**

It is important to consider all the factors that affect children's learning and development. Your focus should be on the finding out about each child's individual needs and routines from home, and what they are interested in and what they can do.

So how can the practitioner make use of this card?

1. Reading the statements on side one of the card, and reflecting on how they as individuals support the babies and young children to feel safe and protected, whilst allowing for choices to be made

2. Looking at the questions on side two of the card – can the practitioner answer the questions, based on the effective practice shown in the top box?

The Challenges and Dilemmas are useful for training purposes – it may be that these could be used as a focus for discussion in your staff meetings. Childminders on a Network could explore these challenges as they meet for support with their Co-ordinator and Early Years teachers. Registered childminders who are not on a Network may attend training, which is open to all early years and childcare providers, to discuss ways in which the challenges may be addressed in their own homes.

At the bottom of the card on side one, you will see reference to Every Child Matters, and the outcome that applies to this card. It is Enjoy and Achieve. Therefore you will see that the welfare requirements linked to this card are included by reference to the outcome.

At the bottom of the card on side two, you will see reference to KEEP, and the statement from KEEP that applies to this card. It is 'Practice in meeting all children's needs, learning styles and interests'. You can order your own copy of the KEEP document from DfES publications department (telephone) 0845 6022260 reference 1201-2005 G

By accessing the CD-ROM, you will find the section on Effective Practice – Observation, Assessment and Planning.

The section covers –

Key Messages

Observation, assessment and planning all support children's development and learning. Planning starts with observing children in order to understand and consider their current interests, development and learning.

■ Observation describes the process of watching the children in our care, listening to them and taking note of what we see and hear

- We assess children's progress by analysing our observations and deciding what they tell us. We also need to find out about children's care and learning needs from their parents, and from these we can identify the children's requirements, interests, current development and learning

- We plan for the next steps in children's development and learning. Much of this needs to be done on the basis of what we have found out from our own observations and assessments as well as information from parents.

So, we need to consider HOW you can effectively observe, assess and plan for each child.

Childminders care for children in a home environment where many varied experiences can be offered. Being in sole charge of children may lead a childminder to wonder how they can take 'time out' to observe the children. Use of post-it's or labels to quickly note something significant that a child has been observed doing is a sensible approach – these brief comments can be added to the child's main records or diary for a fuller picture of how the child is developing – remember to date the notes, and write the child's name on the notes too!

You may consider meeting up with other childminders at drop in sessions, and ask for others to assist whilst you observe a child or all the children in your care.

Whether you are a registered childminder or work in a group setting, you need to understand why your observations are important and why they need to be written. The purpose of making written records is to see what changes are occurring in individual children, if they are progressing, and if any problems are emerging. Through these records, the practitioner can monitor each child as he/she progresses and develops. We must be clear about this – your written observations are not intended to 'grade' children as in school assessments. It is about providing updated information to inform parents of their child's development.

Think about the following –

How are you going to find time within your working day to write your observations? Work together as a team to allow everyone opportunities to make their observations – this will need a flexible approach!

Consider what you are writing – make your observations factual descriptions of what you actually observed.

Remember issues around confidentiality – not sharing written records of children with anyone other than the parents, unless they have given you permission to do so.

By sharing records with parents – showing them how you know about their child's abilities and interests, you and the parents will be able to support the next stage of development. Remember that the parents have a central role in their child's life – they are the main carers and educators.

What skills do you need to be a good observer?

- Looking

- Listening

- Recording

- Thinking

- Questioning.

We need to know what we are **looking** for. Make use of the cards in the EYFS pack and the CD ROM to help you with this. We must pay attention (**listen**) to the interactions of the individual child with different adults and between different children. We can note (**record**) accurate significant features of a child's responses, behaviour, learning and development at the time of the observation. Following the observation, we **think** about what we have seen and this leads to assessing and planning. We may sometimes need to ask **questions** in order to clarify, confirm or reject ideas about what we have observed.

There are several types of observations and the method you choose will depend on what else is going on at the time of the observation. Most observations will be carried out while you are playing and working directly with the babies and young children. At other times you may note something significant – or it may be that you have planned to stand back and watch a child making a more detailed written observation. This type of observation may last for a few minutes.

Two points to remember –

Remember to involve children wherever possible – the United Nations Convention on the Rights of the Child (UNCRC) (Article 12) states the right of the child to express an opinion and to have that opinion taken into account in any matter or procedure affecting the child.

Other than Article 12, the UNCRC have articles that are relevant to all five Every Child Matters outcomes. These are –

Article One

Everyone under 18 years of age has all the rights stated in the UN Convention on the rights of the Child.

Article Two

The Convention applies to everyone, whatever their nation, race, colour, sex, religion, abilities, opinion, wealth or social position.

Article Three

All organisations concerned with children should work towards what is best for each child.

Article Four

Government shall take all necessary steps to make these rights available to all children.

Article Six

All children have the right to life. Governments should ensure that children survive and develop healthily.

Article Twenty-two

Refugee children have the right to protection and assistance and the same rights as other children wherever they are or whatever their circumstances.

If you want a copy of the leaflet that shows further detail of the links between UNCRC and Every Child Matters, go to www.unicef.org.uk/tz

Remember that parents know their child well. They need to be able to share their views and observations with practitioners and become a part of the whole process of assessment for their child.

So what do we mean by assessment?

This is a process of thinking and reviewing what we know about the child's well-being, learning and development. Our 'formative' assessments, ie those which, based on our observations, guide our everyday planning, help us to plan for the next steps.

Summative assessment is simply a summary of all the formative assessments carried out over a long period and makes statements about the child's progress.

The EYFS Profile is a summative assessment completed at the end of the EYFS for each child. It summarises the child's progress towards the Early Learning Goals.

Where they may be concerns about a child, a Common Assessment Framework allows various agencies to communicate to work in the best interests of the child and the family. How does this work?

The Common Assessment Framework (CAF) is about integrated working.

Nationally, the CAF process will ensure that families are not passed around different agencies, but that agencies work together to meet children's needs. The form that can be completed is not a referral form – it is a means of identifying a child's needs and allowing agencies to co-operate in working with the child and the family. This process comes about when people who work closely with children identify a concern or notes a problem for a child. The family needs to be engaged in a dialogue that produces a holistic picture of the child's situation, evidence to underpin the concerns and agreement with family about what needs to be done in the child's best interests.

Your local authority will offer training to those who are interested in the CAF process, but all settings should be aware of CAF, and how this may be used in the setting.

Our observations on children are the starting point. By looking, listening and noting what has been seen and/or heard, the practitioner can make an assessment – analysing the observation and deciding what the observation tells you about the child. Planning is the final step – considering what experiences or opportunities are necessary for the child, giving consideration to the learning environment, resources, routines, and crucially, the role of the practitioner.

Understanding that planning covers the long, medium and short term is important for every practitioner.

Long term planning relates to the overall guidance for the children

contained in the EYFS document. You need to think about how you ensure that you cover all areas of learning and development and the principles of EYFS. As you organise your long term plans, identify the links between the different areas of learning and development and the principles. Consider how you are going to balance indoor and outdoor activities (to include quiet times/areas) throughout the day.

Long term planning helps you to focus on your medium term plans, which usually cover, in some detail, the overall programme fro anything between 2- 6 weeks at a time. Within these plans, think about the types of experiences appropriate to your setting – linking to the principles of EYFS. Consider how your overall daily routines meet the children's needs, and how you make best use of your resources for all the children in your setting.

In the short term, you are giving more thought to the day-to- day needs of children. You are able to focus on what specific needs the children have, based on your observations, and how these needs will be met. Your plans are likely to include the resources you need and how you intend to put the principles into practice for the children. All practitioners need to be familiar with the principles of EYFS and be guided by them in their work with all children.

The theme of Enabling Environments has 4 commitments. We have considered Observation, Assessment and Planning in detail. The other 3 commitments are –

Supporting Every Child

The environment supports every child's learning through planned experiences and activities that are challenging but achievable.

Key Messages for Supporting Every Child are:

■ In addition to their genetic make-up, the environments in which children grow up also have a strong influence on what they do and can accomplish

■ Each child's experiences add up to a unique combination that they carry with them on their learning journey

■ Children's needs differ according to genetic factors, cultural practices, social trends and their many experiences. When these needs are clearly identified we can create an environment that enhances learning and development

■ Children must be able to relate new experiences to the unique blend of experiences that they have already encountered

■ Most children will follow the same broad routes but must be able to find their own pathways along the way

■ It is important to keep the learning journey smooth at times of transition when changes are greatest

■ Working together with children, families and other professionals enable settings to create learning environments that best provide for the needs of all children

■ The learning environment should support children working and playing together, as well as supporting good relationships between adults and children

■ Working together with parents helps practitioners to identify what is necessary for each child at any time

■ Working together with other professionals and community groups, in the interests of young children, enables settings to create contexts for learning that benefit all children.

The Learning Environment

A rich and varied environment supports children's learning and development. It gives them the confidence to explore and learn in secure and safe, yet challenging, indoor and outdoor spaces.

Key Messages for The Learning Environment are:

■ Babies, toddlers and young children thrive best in an environment that supports and promotes their active learning and development

■ Young children require space, indoors and outdoors, where they can be active or quiet, and where they can think, dream and watch others

■ The space needs to be appropriate for the age and the development of all the children so that they can have suitable access to it and can interact within it

■ The space needs to be secure, appropriately heated and aired and free from hazards

■ There needs to be well-organised areas and resources, both natural and manufactured, which are accessible to the children

■ There should be opportunities for a range of activities such as soft play, paint mixing, growing plants, mark making, looking at books, reading stories, or exploring the properties of materials such as clay, sand or water

■ The space both indoors and outdoors should preferably be available all the time so children can choose activities and follow their interests

■ The outdoor space needs to offer shade and shelter, and children should have opportunities to experience changing seasons and the passing of time

■ In deciding what is an 'appropriate environment', it is important to understand the way babies, toddlers and young children learn, and to provide for the age and the stage of the children concerned

■ There is no ideal environment, as babies' and young children's interests change, and the environment should change in response to these changing interests .

The Wider Context

Working in partnership with other settings, other professionals and with individuals and groups in the community, supports children's

development and progress towards the five outcomes of Every Child Matters.

Key Messages for The Wider Context are:

■ It is important that the benefits of having a diverse system of childcare providers outweigh the challenges of coping with the differences between them, which can unsettle children and affect their ability to thrive

■ Where experiences are different but complementary, they contribute positively to children's learning and development

■ Children will respond in different ways to changes within their experience

■ Practitioners must work with families to link and support children's learning and development in the different settings that they attend

■ Partnership between providers and other agencies in the local community enhance practice and create consistency and quality in the care and education of all children

■ Effective communication with families, practitioners in other settings and with other professionals is central to ensuring continuity and progression in learning.

Learning and Development
4.1 Play and Exploration

Look at the headings on side one of the card –

■ Learning through experience

■ Adult involvement

■ Context for learning.

These headings are specific to this card. The commitment (statement) that applies to the card is clearly shown at the top –

Children's play reflects their wide ranging and varied interests and preoccupations. **In their play, children learn at their highest level.** Play with peers is important for children's development.

Why are some of the words printed in bold?

These are the key words that apply to this card. If you look on the other cards, you will see that they also have bold print to identify the key words for those cards.

So, let's focus on **in their play, children learn at their highest level**

Play is natural for most children – children may play alone or with others. The player is in control. Children can learn naturally through play without fear of failure. Through play, children will build on experiences they have had and may use their play to try things out and solve problems. They may express their fears through play. Play and exploration in early years settings means that children are able to choose activities where they can engage with other children or adults or sometimes play alone. During those activities they learn by first hand experience – by actively 'doing'.

So, how can the practitioner make use of this card?

1. Reading the statements on side one of the card, and reflecting on how

they as individuals support babies and young children in forming close, emotional relationships

2. Looking at the questions on side two of the card – can the practitioner answer the questions, based on the effective practice shown in the top box?

The Challenges and Dilemmas are useful for training purposes – it may be that these could be used as a focus for discussion in your staff meetings. Childminders on a Network could explore these challenges as they meet for support with their Co-ordinator and Early Years teachers. Registered childminders who are not on a Network may attend training, which is open to all early years and childcare providers, to discuss ways in which the challenges may be addressed in their own homes.

At the bottom of the card on side one, you will see reference to Every Child Matters, and the outcome that applies to this card. It is Enjoy and Achieve. Therefore you will see that the welfare requirements linked to this card are included by reference to the outcome.

At the bottom of the card on side two, you will see reference to KEEP, and the statement from KEEP that applies to this card. It is 'Understanding of the individual and diverse ways that children develop and learn'. You can order your own copy of the KEEP document from the DfES publications department (telephone)0845 6022260 Reference 2101-2005 G.

By accessing the CD-ROM, you will find the section on Effective Practice – Play and Exploration.

The section covers –

Key Messages

- Children learn through first hand experience, in activities they have chosen

- Play can involve a child playing alone, alongside another child, or co-operatively with another child/ children/adult

- Children are given opportunities to test their ideas, themselves, their relationships and materials

- Play and exploration promotes brain development

- Children and adults can make and learn from their mistakes

- Play fosters imagination and flexibility of mind, promoting children's ability to be 'players' now and in the future

- Children's competencies and confidence are developed through play

- During play, children's concepts, skills, attitudes and achievements are extended

- Effective practitioners evaluate the extent to which they provide for all children's learning dispositions

- Rich, enabling environments, with sufficient and appropriate safe space and equipment, are provided

- Practitioners should allow children to dictate the pace, length and focus of activities and any interventions should be subtly supportive

- Loving, sensitive key people recognise and provide for babies' and young children's fascination with and curiosity about what is going on in their worlds.

So, why is play and exploration so important?

- making choices and decisions

- using one's own ideas and imagination

- experimenting

- trying out new behaviours and practising old ones

- practising skills and learning new ones

- exercising, developing and co-ordinating body, mind and brain

- adapting or transforming knowledge, attitudes and skills

- negotiating

- following an interest or line of enquiry

- engaging in a 'what if?' activity

- making up rules and changing them

- making mistakes

- demonstrating one's competence in many areas of development

- setting one's own goals

- trying to emulate someone else

- using symbols

- making sense of puzzling situations, events or equipment

- becoming and being confident and enjoying challenges

- having fun with friends and/or familiar adults

- learning how to be a 'player'.

When we think about children's dispositions for learning, we can consider Margaret Carr's work in New Zealand (2001). She suggests that there are 5 domains of learning disposition –

- taking an interest

- being involved

- persisting with difficulty or uncertainty

- communicating with others

- taking responsibility.

Margaret Carr places these domains into three parts, which are familiar to many people –

Being ready, willing and able.

The theme of Learning and Development has 4 commitments. We have considered Play and Exploration in some detail. Two other commitments are –

Active Learning

Children learn best though physical and mental challenges. Active learning involves other people, objects, ideas and events that engage and involve children for sustained periods.

Key Messages for Active Learning are:

■ Babies and young children learn by actively investigating the world around them and through social activity with people

■ Children's interactions enable them to construct ideas and create a framework for thinking and learning that helps them to develop as learners

■ When children are actively involved in learning, they are developing the mental structures that help them to think and move on. These are sometimes known as schemas

■ Practitioners contribute to children's active learning by creating the climate and conditions to promote their involvement

■ Making decisions is important in children's learning, putting them in control and enabling them to match their play with what they want to achieve

■ Children develop autonomy as learners by making and following through their decisions about their learning

■ Engaging children in active learning depends on understanding and building on what each child is familiar with, knows, and can do

■ The range of activities available should enable all children to find something that is relevant to engage and sustain their interest

■ Good working relationships with parents help practitioners to provide inviting contexts that children recognise and can learn from.

Creativity and Critical Thinking

When children have opportunities to play with ideas in different situations and with a variety of resources, they discover connections and come to new and better understandings and ways of doing things. Adult support in this process enhances their ability to think critically and ask questions.

Key Messages for Creativity and Critical Thinking are:

■ Creativity emerges when children become absorbed in exploring the world around them

■ Directing children's attention during play often disturbs a child's flow of ideas but adults can, and should, contribute by following children's leads

■ Sharing children's thinking makes adults aware of children's interests and understandings and enables them to foster development of knowledge and ideas

■ Children discover new meanings when they explore possibilities and create new connections between people, places and things

■ Creativity fosters critical thinking by allowing children to review and reinvent.

The areas of Learning and Development

This is the final section within the set of cards. The section has an explanation of the 6 areas of learning and development (card 4.4), and then 6 separate cards, which consider all areas of learning and development under the headings of –

■ Personal, Social and Emotional Development

■ Communication, Language and Literacy

■ Problem Solving, Reasoning and Numeracy

■ Knowledge and Understanding of the World

■ Physical Development

■ Creative Development.

The EYFS is made up of these 6 areas of learning and development. Each area is connected to another and are equally important. All of the 6 areas of learning and development are underpinned by the principles of the EYFS.

Practitioners who have worked with the Birth – Three framework will be familiar already with the headings of development matters, look listen and note, effective practice and planning and resourcing. They will be less familiar with linking these headings under the 6 areas of learning that foundation stage practitioners are most familiar with. These two documents have been brought together for the EYFS along with elements of the National Standards of Care to enable practitioners to support the development, learning and care of babies and young children. This is not a curriculum – it a statutory framework that is designed to assist practitioners in their day-to day work with young children.

Concerns have been expressed that, while the sections in the Practice Guidance Book are intended to support practitioners in their work with babies and young children, there will be a tendency to use the sections as checklists. Many practitioners feel that this is the way to 'prove' to Ofsted that they are doing everything within the EYFS for each child. Many practitioners have expressed concerns that some Ofsted inspectors may see the sections as checklists to be completed for each child. This became a concern with the Birth – Three Framework. There were reports that inspectors in some areas had unrealistic expectations – they did not regard the Framework in a holistic way and there were reports of inspectors asking to see the 'plans for learning'.

It is hoped that nationally,

1. all inspectors will appreciate the EYFS for it's holistic approach, and not be drawn towards regarding the document as a curriculum for babies and young children.

2. all inspectors will receive appropriate training to be able to explore with settings how they are effectively implementing the EYFS in a holistic way.

3. inspectors who currently have less knowledge of settings where children have, for example, specific needs, gain that knowledge to ensure an accurate inspection takes place that really reflects the setting.

For each of the 6 areas of learning, let's focus on an age range to explore in detail what you need to consider with children of –

Birth – 11 months –
we will consider Personal, Social and Emotional Development

8 – 20 months (8 months – 1 year 8 months) -
we will consider Communication, Language and Literacy

16 months – 26 months (1 year 4 months – 2 years 2 months) –
we will consider Problem Solving, Reasoning and Numeracy

22 months – 36 months (1 year 10 months – 3 years) –
we will consider Knowledge and Understanding of the World

30 months – 50 months (2 years 6 months – 4 years 2 months) –
we will consider Physical Development

40 months – 60 months (3 years 4 months - 5 years +) –
we will consider Creative Development

Personal, Social and Emotional Development

Let's look at the card from the pack, headed –

■ Learning and Development

■ Personal, Social and Emotional Development.

Under the heading on side one of the card, you will see the requirements of this area of learning.

Children must be provided with experiences and support, which will help them to develop a positive sense of themselves and of others; social skills; and a positive disposition to learn. Providers must ensure support for children's emotional well being to help them to know themselves and what they can do.

At the bottom of side one of the card you will see the heading of personal, social and emotional development highlighted in red, to remind you of the area this card represents. The two boxes show the aspects of this area of learning, which are –

■ Dispositions and attitudes

■ Self-confidence and self-esteem

■ Making relationships

■ Behaviour and self-control

■ Self-care

■ Sense of community.

You need to familiarise yourself with these aspect headings, and the statements in the second box, which explain what personal, social and emotional development means for children between birth and five years of age.

On side two of the card, the boxes show links to other cards in your packs – Positive Relationships and Enabling Environments.

(You may have noticed that the **colours** for the two headings on side two of the card do not match the colours for Positive Relationships and Enabling Environments. The green and purple colours are the wrong way round, but the content of the boxes is correct. This error in the colour has been noted by the Primary National Strategy and in the next print of the EYFS pack, the colours will be correct.)

So, how do you make the links to the areas of positive relationships and enabling environments?

Rather than just read the bullet points in the boxes, turn them into questions, to allow everyone in the setting to consider HOW they can effectively implement this area of learning and development –

1. In what ways do we form warm, caring attachments with children in the group?

2. How do we establish constructive relationships with parents and workers from other agencies?

3. What opportunities do we offer to give encouragement to children – do we act as role models who value differences and take account of different needs and expectations?

4. Do we plan for opportunities for children to play and learn, sometimes alone and sometimes in groups of various sizes?

5. Do we have a key worker system, and do all practitioners recognise the benefits?

6. How do we make sure that there is time and space for children to concentrate on activities and experiences and develop their own interests?

7. What positive images do we provide that challenge children's thinking and help them to embrace differences?

8. What opportunities do we offer for play and learning that acknowledge children's particular religious beliefs and cultural backgrounds?

In the Learning and Development box on side two of the card, you will see ways in which you may help children to achieve personally, emotionally and socially. These points link into your

Practice guidance books on pages 22-38. Let's look at this section of the book –

The information in this section is designed to help you observe, plan and assess your activities with children based on their individual development and needs.

On pages 24-38, you will see that there are four columns that represent the cycle of children's development in the area of personal, emotional and social development, for all the ages between 0-5 years. These ages are shown in months – refer back to page 8 of this book, to see the ages referred to in years, as well as months.

The sections **are not** intended to be all you need to consider – we know that children will do different things at different rates.

We must guard against using these sections as checklists.

On page 24 onwards of the Practice Guidance Book, we can see that, in addition to the ages down the left hand side, we have four headings across the top. These are –

■ Development matters

■ Look, listen and note

■ Effective practice

■ Planning and resourcing.

What do these headings mean?

In the Practice Guidance Book, the information is clear –

Development matters 'identify the developing knowledge, skills, understanding and attitudes that children will need if they are to achieve the Early Learning Goals BY the end of the EYFS. It is important to note that children will not necessarily progress sequentially through the stages, since these do not represent age-related goals. By the end of the end of the EYFS, some children will have exceeded the goals, while others will be working towards some or all of them'.

Look, listen and note guides the practitioner in their 'observations of children which helps them to assess the progress children are making. Observations help practitioners to decide

where children are in their learning and development and to plan what to do.

Effective practice guides practitioners towards ' forming a view of where each child is in their learning, where they need to go, and the most effective practice to support them in getting there. The guidance on effective practice to support children's development is based on the EYFS principles and the examples given illustrate just some of the possibilities'.

Planning and resourcing reminds the practitioner that 'good planning is the key to making children's learning effective, exciting, varied and progressive. It enables practitioners to build up knowledge about how individual children learn and make progress. Plans should be flexible enough to adapt to circumstances'. If you refer to card –

> 3.1 Theme - Enabling Environments Commitment, Observation, Planning and Assessment.

you will find further guidance. This card helps you to make informed decisions about each child's progress, and suggests ways in which you can plan the next steps to meet their development and learning needs. This is your assessment of the child's learning.

PERSONAL, SOCIAL AND EMOTIONAL DEVELOPMENT – birth – 11 months

On pages 24, 27, 30, 33, 35, 37 of your Practice Guidance Book, you will find the birth – 11 months sections that relate to dispositions and attitudes, self-confidence and self-esteem, making relationships, behaviour and self-control, self care and sense of community.

What do you need to do next?

Read the sections for this age group that deal with

- Development matters

- Look, listen and note

- Effective practice

- Planning and resourcing.

Then consider the following for the babies –

Dispositions and attitudes

Do you –

- say or sing made-up rhymes or songs while stroking or pointing to the babies' hands, feet or cheeks?

- respond to and build on babies' expressions, actions, and gestures?

- find out what babies like and dislike through talking to their parents?

Self-confidence and self-esteem

Do you –

- recognise that young babies will find comfort from 'snuggling in' with a variety of objects and people?

- talk to a young baby when you cannot give them your direct attention, so that they are aware of your interest and your presence nearby?

Making relationships

Do you –

- ensure that the key person is available to greet a young baby at the beginning of the session, and to hand them over to the parents at the end of a session, so that the baby is supported appropriately and communication with parents is maintained?

- engage in playful interactions that encourage young babies to respond to, or mimic, adults?

- ensure all staff have detailed information about the home language experiences of all children?

Under this heading, you will find it useful to consider the additional information and guidance materials in Early Support. You will see references to Early Support on the cards in your EYFS pack. This programme is a government initiative from the DfES (Department for Education and Skills), Sure Start and the Department of Health. The purpose of the programme is to improve the delivery of services to disabled children under the age of 3 years, and their families. Under the heading of Making Relationships for this age group, the Early Support programme suggests that you consider the following –

- When you talk to babies, make sure you are face to face

- It is important to share quiet moments together. Babies enjoy the intimacy of being close and looking at each other. They are learning about people and themselves as they do so

- Comment when babies move or make sounds, for example, when a baby burps, you could say 'Do you feel better now?'

- Touch is very important. Stroking, tickling and cuddles all help babies to become aware of you and enjoy being with you and listening to you

- Keep close and encourage babies to feel or look at your face. Let them feel your lips when you are talking or making play noises. Young babies find faces very interesting

- Copy the sounds, mouth movements and facial expressions that babies use. Sometimes they will copy you too

- Copy any sounds and gestures babies make while they are watching you

- Watch out for how babies show frustration or discomfort and for how this changes once they are comforted and satisfied. When babies cry, lift them up and reassure them

- Rock babies rhythmically to songs and music

- Watch out for how babies show that they have had enough and want to stop interaction. They may start to cry, stiffen, lean away from you or close their eyes and mouth. Give the two of you a break – they will show you when they are ready to play again

- Call a baby's name gently as you approach them and say 'Up you come!' Wait to see if they can show you that they want to be picked up

- 'Mirror' a baby's feelings through your voice intonation, body movement and facial expressions. This shows them that you are tuning into their moods.

Behaviour and self-control

Do you –

- find out as much as you can from parents about young babies before they join the setting, so that the routines you follow are familiar and comforting?

Self-care

Do you –

- encourage babies gradually to share control of food and drink? This provides opportunities for sensory learning and increased independence

- talk to babies about different people and places they know?

We have considered the birth – 11 months age group for the aspects of Personal, Social and Emotional Development. There is further information on the aspects for the other age groups within the EYFS pack and on the CD-ROM.

COMMUNICATION, LANGUAGE and LITERACY

Let's look at the card from the pack, headed –

- Learning and Development

- Communication, Language and Literacy.

Under the heading on side one of the card, you will see the requirements of this area of learning.

Children's learning and competence in communicating, speaking and listening, being read to and beginning to read and write must be supported. They must be provided with opportunity and encouragement to use their skills in a range of situations and for a range of purposes, and be supported in developing the confidence and disposition to do so.

At the bottom of side one of the card you will see the heading of communication, language and literacy highlighted in red, to remind you of the area this card represents. The two boxes show the aspects of this area of learning, which are –

- Language for communication

- Language for thinking

- Linking sounds and letters

- Reading

- Writing

- Handwriting.

You need to familiarise yourself with these aspect headings, and the statements in the second box, which explain what communication, language and literacy means for children between birth and five years of age.

On side two of the card, the boxes show links to other cards in your packs – Positive Relationships and Enabling Environments.

(As with the other 6 cards under Learning and Development, you may have noticed that the **colours** for the two headings on side two of the card do not match the colours for Positive Relationships and Enabling Environments. The green and purple colours are the wrong way round, but the content of the boxes is correct. This error in the colour has been noted by the Primary National Strategy and in the next print of the EYFS pack, the colours will be correct.)

So, how do you make the links to the areas of positive relationships and enabling environments?

Rather than just read the bullet points in the boxes, turn them into questions, to allow everyone in the setting to consider HOW they can effectively implement this area of learning and development –

1. How do we help children to communicate their thoughts, ideas and feelings and build up relationships with adults and with each other?

2. What daily opportunities do the children have to share and enjoy a wide range of fiction and non-fiction books, rhymes, music, songs, poetry and stories?

3. Do we allow children to see us reading and writing? Do we encourage children to experiment with writing for themselves through making marks, personal writing symbols and conventional script?

4. Do we identify and respond to any particular difficulties in children's language development at an early stage?

5. Have we planned our environment so that it is rich in signs, symbols, notices, numbers, words, rhymes, books, pictures, music and songs that take into account children's different interests, understandings, home backgrounds and cultures?

6. What alternative systems do we have in place for children who may need to use other forms of communication which will provide opportunities for them to record their ideas and to gain access to texts in an alternative way, for example, through ICT?

7. Do we allow time for children to develop spoken language through sustained conversations between children and adults, both one-to one and in small groups and between the children themselves? Do we allow children time to initiate their conversations, respect their thinking time and silences and help them to develop interactions?

8. Are we sensitive to the needs of children learning English as a second language? Do we enable them to use their home language when appropriate and ensure close team work between ourselves, parents and bilingual workers so that the children's developing use of English and other languages support each other?

In the Learning and Development box on side two of the card, you will see ways in which you may help children under this area of learning. These points link into your Practice guidance books on pages 39-60. Lets look at this section of the book.

The information in this section is designed to help you observe, plan and assess your activities with children based on their individual development and needs.

On pages 41-60, you will see that there are four columns that represent the cycle of children's development in the area of communication, language and literacy, for all the ages between 0-5 years. These ages are shown in months – refer back to page 8 of this book, to see the ages referred to in years, as well as months.

The sections **are not** intended to be all you need to consider – we know that children will do different things at different rates.

We must guard against using these sections as checklists.

On page 41 onwards of the Practice Guidance Book, we can see that, in addition to the ages down the left hand side, we have four headings across the top. These are –

■ Development matters

■ Look, listen and note

■ Effective practice

■ Planning and resourcing.

What do these headings mean?

In the Practice Guidance Book, the information is clear –

Development matters 'identify the developing knowledge, skills, understanding and attitudes that children will need if they are to achieve the Early Learning Goals BY the end of the EYFS. It is important to note that children will not necessarily progress sequentially through the stages, since these do not represent age-related goals. By the end of the end of the EYFS, some children will have exceeded the goals, while others will be working towards some or all of them'.

Look, listen and note guides the practitioner in their 'observations of children which helps them to assess the progress children are making. Observations help practitioners to decide where children are in their learning and development and to plan what to do.

Effective practice guides practitioners towards ' forming a view of where each child is in their learning, where they need to go, and the most effective practice to support them in getting there. The guidance on effective practice to support children's development is based on the EYFS principles and the examples given illustrate just some of the possibilities'.

Planning and resourcing reminds the practitioner that 'good planning is the key to making children's learning effective, exciting, varied and progressive. It enables practitioners to build up knowledge about how individual children learn and make progress. Plans should be flexible enough to adapt to circumstances'. If you refer to card –

   3.2 Theme - Enabling Environments
   Commitment, Observation,
   Planning and Assessment.

you will find further guidance. This card helps you to make informed decisions about each child's progress, and suggests ways in which you can plan the next steps to meet their development and learning needs. This is your assessment of the child's learning.

COMMUNICATION, LANGUAGE AND LITERACY 8 - 20 months (8 months - 1 year 8 months)

On pages 41, 47, 50, 53, 57, 59 of your Practice Guidance Book, you will find the 8 months – 20 months sections that relate to language for communication, language for thinking, linking sounds and letters, reading, writing and handwriting.

What do you need to do next?

Read the sections for this age group that deal with

■ Development matters

■ Look, listen and note

■ Effective practice

■ Planning and resourcing.

Then consider the following for the young children –

Language for children

Do you –

■ try to 'tune in' to the different messages young babies are trying to convey?

■ find out from parents about greetings used in English and in languages other than English – do you encourage staff, parents and children to become familiar with them?

■ recognise and value the importance of all languages spoken and written by parents, staff and children?

Under this heading, you will find it useful to consider the additional information and guidance materials in Early Support. You will see references to Early Support on the cards in your EYFS pack. This programme is a government initiative from the DfES (Department for Education and Skills), Sure Start and the Department of Health. The purpose of the programme is to improve the delivery of services to disabled children under the age of

3 years, and their families. Under the heading of Communication, Language and Literacy for this age group, the Early Support programme suggests that you consider the following –

■ Watch children and think about how they tell you what they want, for example, by cuddling in when they want more cuddles, wriggling their fingers when they want to be picked up, and crying to show that they are uncomfortable or wet

■ Respond to children's attempts to communicate so that they know they have succeeded

■ Put into words what you think children are trying to tell you

■ Play games such as peek-a-boo and recite rhymes such as 'pat a cake' and 'round and round the garden', using associated actions and gestures

■ Play give-and-take games where toys and objects are exchanged

■ Share books to promote shared attention – books help you to know you are focused on the same things as you talk about them

■ Tell children the names of things and people they see in books and all around them

■ Recast what children are trying to communicate by taking their incomplete utterances and giving them back the language they need. When a child pushes something away, you might say "You don't like that, do you?"

■ Copy the first attempts at words that children make so that they can see and hear the full version. When a child says "mo" you might say "More? You want more?"

Language for thinking

Do you –

■ talk to babies about what you are doing, so that they will link words with actions, for example, when you are preparing lunch?

Linking sounds with letters

Do you –

■ share the fun of discovery and value babies' attempts at words, for example, by pocking up a doll in response to "baba?"

Under this heading, you will find it useful to consider the additional information and guidance materials in Early Support. Under the heading of Communication, Language and Literacy for this age group, the Early Support programme suggests that you consider the following –

■ Watch and interpret children's behaviour and praise word-like sounds

■ Play peek-a-boo and action games to support babies' attention, sometimes over long periods of time. They also help to develop anticipation and offer children many opportunities to imitate and join in, which they will now do increasingly

■ Imitate the noises babies make, such as laughter and other vocalisations

■ Use bubbles to encourage repetition of the 'pop, pop, pop' sound you make as the bubble bursts

■ Avoid correcting children's attempts at words. Simply repeat what they are trying to say, correctly

■ Respond to children's attempts at words by commenting on them, for example, when a child says "dogon", you say "Yes, the dog has gone home. He might came back later".

Reading

Do you –

■ tell stories and read stories, looking and interacting with young babies?

■ let children handle books and draw attention to pictures?

Writing

Do you –

■ talk to babies about the patterns and marks they make?

Handwriting

Do you –

■ describe the movements young babies make as they move round and round, or ride a push-a-long toy in a straight line?

We have considered the 8- 20 months (8 months – 1 year 8 months) age group for the aspects of Communication, Language and Literacy. There is further information on the aspects for the other age groups within the EYFS pack and on the CD ROM. At the end of the EYFS, within this area of development, under linking sounds and letters, children should be able to 'hear and say sounds in words in the order in which they occur'. This wording has been changed as an early learning goal from the wording currently used in the Foundation Stage. There has been much discussion and debate around developing children's language.

The recommendations of the Independent Review of the Teaching of Early Reading carried out by Jim Rose have been incorporated into the EYFS and the Primary Framework. The whole of the Rose Review can be accessed through www.teachernet. gov.uk/publications. The main recommendations are –

■ It is very important to develop children's positive attitudes to literacy, in the broadest sense and from the earliest stages, in partnership with parents and carers

■ Best practice for beginner readers provides them a rich curriculum that fosters all four independent stages of language

■ Good phonics teaching is systematic, multi-sensory and interactive in order to capture children's interests and sustain motivation and reinforce learning

■ High quality, systematic phonic work should be taught discreetly and should normally start by the age of five years, taking full account of professional judgements of children's developing abilities.

These recommendations are embedded in Communication, Language and Literacy. It is stressed that a more systematic approach to teaching reading does not mean 'drilling' babies or very children in phonics. Most of the work up to the age of five years will be about supporting children's phonological awareness; the general ability to attend to the sounds and rhythms of language. The debate around this is on-going.

PROBLEM SOLVING, REASONING and NUMERACY

Let's look at the card from the pack, headed –

■ Learning and Development

■ Problem Solving, Reasoning and Numeracy.

Under the heading on side one of the card, you will see the requirements of this area of learning.

Children must be supported in developing their understanding of Problem Solving, Reasoning and Numeracy in a broad range of contexts in which they can explore, enjoy, learn, practise and talk about their developing and understanding. They must be provided with opportunities to practise these skills and to gain confidence and competence in their use.

At the bottom of side one of the card you will see the heading of problem solving, reasoning and numeracy highlighted in red, to remind you of the area this card represents. The two boxes show the aspects of this area of learning, which are –

■ Numbers as labels and for counting

■ Calculating

■ Shape, space and measurement.

You need to familiarise your self with these aspect headings, and the statements in the second box, which explain what problem solving, reasoning and numeracy means for children between birth and five years of age.

On side two of the card, the boxes show links to other cards in your packs – Positive Relationships and Enabling Environments.

(As with the other 6 cards under Learning and Development, you may have noticed that the colours for the two headings on side two of the card do not match the colours for Positive Relationships and Enabling Environments. The green and purple colours are the wrong way round, but the content of the boxes is correct. This error in the colour has been noted by the Primary National Strategy and in the next print of the EYFS pack, the colours will be correct)

So, how do you make the links to the areas of positive relationships and enabling environments?

Rather than just read the bullet points in the boxes, turn them into questions, to allow everyone in the setting to consider HOW they can effectively implement this area of learning and development –

1. How do we give children sufficient time, space and encouragement to discover and use new words and mathematical ideas, concepts and language during child-initiated activities in their own play?

2. What encouragement do we give children to explore real life problems, to make patterns and to count and match together, for example, ask "How many spoons do we need for everyone in this group to have one?"

3. What systems do we have in place to support children who use a means of communication other than spoken English to develop and understand specific mathematical language while valuing knowledge of Problem Solving, Reasoning and Numeracy in the language or communication system that they use at home?

4. Do we value children's own practical explorations of this area of learning?

5. Do we maximise the potential of our outdoor environment, for example, for children to discover things about shape, distance and measures, through their physical activities?

6. Do we exploit the mathematical potential of the indoor environment for example, by enabling children to discover things about numbers, counting and calculating through practical situations?

7. How do we make sure that we have mathematical resources readily available both indoors and outside?

In the Learning and Development box on side two of the card, you will see ways in which you may help children under this area of learning. These points link into your Practice guidance books on pages 61- 74. Let's look at this section of the book –

The information in this section is designed to help you observe, plan and assess your activities with children based on their individual development and needs.

On pages 63-74, you will see that there are four columns that represent the cycle of children's development in the area of communication, language and literacy, for all the ages between 0-5 years. These ages are shown in months – refer back to page 8 of this book, to see the ages referred to in years, as well as months.

The sections **are not** intended to be all you need to consider – we know that children will do different things at different rates.

We must guard against using these sections as checklists.

On page 63 onwards of the Practice Guidance Book, we can see that, in addition to the ages down the left hand side, we have four headings across the top. These are –

■ Development matters

■ Look, listen and note

■ Effective practice

■ Planning and resourcing.

What do these headings mean?

In the Practice Guidance Book, the information is clear –

Development matters 'identify the developing knowledge, skills, understanding and attitudes that children will need if they are to achieve the Early Learning Goals BY the end of the EYFS. It is important to note that children will not necessarily progress sequentially through the stages, since these do not represent age-related goals. By the end of the end of the EYFS, some children will have exceeded the goals, while others will be working towards some or all of them'.

Look, listen and note guides the practitioner in their 'observations of children which helps them to assess the progress children are making. Observations help practitioners to decide where children are in their learning and development and to plan what to do.

Effective practice guides practitioners towards ' forming a view of where each child is in their learning, where they need to go, and the most effective practice to support them in getting there. The guidance on

effective practice to support children's development is based on the EYFS principles and the examples given illustrate just some of the possibilities'.

Planning and resourcing reminds the practitioner that 'good planning is the key to making children's learning effective, exciting, varied and progressive. It enables practitioners to build up knowledge about how individual children learn and make progress. Plans should be flexible enough to adapt to circumstances'. If you refer to card –

> 3.3 Theme - Enabling Environments Commitment, Observation, Planning and Assessment.

you will find further guidance. This card helps you to make informed decisions about each child's progress, and suggests ways in which you can plan the next steps to meet their development and learning needs. This is your assessment of the child's learning.

PROBLEM SOLVING, REASONING AND NUMERACY 16 – 26 months (1 year 4 months - 2 years 2 months)

On pages 63, 64, 67,70,71 of your Practice Guidance Book, you will find the 16-26 months section that relate to numbers as labels and for counting, calculating, and shape, space and measures.

What do you need to do next?

Read the sections for this age group that deal with

■ Development matters

■ Look, listen and note

■ Effective practice

■ Planning and resourcing.

Then consider the following for the young children –

Numbers as labels and for counting

Do you –

■ use number words in meaningful contexts, for example, "Here's your other mitten. Now we have two"?

■ talk to young children about 'lots' and 'few' as they play?

■ talk about young children's choices and where appropriate, demonstrate how counting help us to find out how many?

■ give opportunities for children to practise one-to-one correspondence in real-life situations?

■ talk about maths in everyday situations, for example, doing up a coat, one hole for each button?

■ tell parents all about the ways children learn about numbers in your setting. Do you have interpreter support or translated materials to support children and families learning English as an additional language?

Calculating

Do you –

■ foster children's ability to classify and compare amounts?

■ use 'tidy up' time to promote logic and reasoning about where things fit in or where they are kept?

Shape, space and measures

Do you –

■ talk to children as they play with water or sand, to encourage them to think about when something is full, empty or hold more?

■ help young children to create different arrangements in the layout of road and rail tracks?

■ highlight patterns in daily activities and routines?

■ help children to touch, see and feel shape through art, music, and dance?

■ encourage children to create their own patterns in art, music and dance?

We have considered the 16 – 26 months (1 year 4 months – 2 years 2 months) age group for the aspects of Problem Solving, Reasoning and Numeracy. There is further information on the aspects for the other age groups within the EYFS pack and on the CD-ROM.

KNOWLEDGE and UNDERSTANDING of the WORLD

Let's look at the card from the pack, headed –

■ Learning and Development

■ Knowledge and Understanding of the World.

Under the heading on side one of the card, you will see the requirements of this area of learning.

Children must be supported in developing the knowledge, skills and understanding that help them to make sense of the world. Their learning must be supported through offering opportunities for them to use a range of tools safely; encounter creatures, people, plants and objects in their natural environments and in real life situations; undertake practical 'experiments' and work with a range of materials.

At the bottom of side one of the card you will see the heading of knowledge and understanding of the world highlighted in red, to remind you of the area this card represents. The two boxes show the aspects of this area of learning, which are –

■ Exploration and investigation

■ Designing and making

■ ICT

■ Time

■ Place

■ Communities.

You need to familiarise your self with these aspect headings, and the statements in the second box, which explain what this area of learning means for children between birth and five years of age.

On side two of the card, the boxes show links to other cards in your packs – Positive Relationships and Enabling Environments.

(As with the other 6 cards under Learning and Development, you may have noticed that the colours for the two headings on side two of the card do not match the colours for Positive Relationships and Enabling Environments. The green and purple colours are the wrong way round, but the content of the boxes is correct. This error in the colour has been noted by the Primary National Strategy and in the next print of the EYFS pack, the colours will be correct.)

So, how do you make the links to the areas of positive relationships and enabling environments?

Rather than just read the bullet points in the boxes, turn them into questions, to allow everyone in the setting to consider HOW they can effectively implement this area of learning and development –

1. How do we use parents' and carers' knowledge to extend children's experiences of the world?

2. What opportunities do we give children to become aware of, explore and question differences in gender, ethnicity, language, religion, culture, special educational needs and disability issues?

3. How do we support children with sensory impairment to ensure that they can enhance their learning about the world around them?

4. Is our environment stimulating? Do we offer a range of activities, which will encourage children's interest and curiosity, both indoors and outside?

5. Do we make effective use of outdoors, including the local neighbourhood?

6. Do we use correct terms so that, for example, children will enjoy naming a 'chrysalis' if we use the correct name?

7. Do we use open-ended questions such as "How can we...?" or "What would happen if...?"

In the Learning and Development box on side two of the card, you will see ways in which you may help children under this area of learning. These points link into your Practice guidance books on pages 75-89. Let's look at this section of the book –

The information in this section is designed to help you observe, plan and assess your activities with children based on their individual development and needs.

On pages 77-89, you will see that there are four columns that represent the cycle of children's development in the area of knowledge and understanding of the world, for all the ages between 0-5 years. These ages are shown in months – refer back to page 8 of this book, to see the ages referred to in years, as well as months.

The sections **are not** intended to be all you need to consider – we know that children will do different things at different rates.

We must guard against using these sections as checklists.

On page 77 onwards of the Practice Guidance Book, we can see that, in addition to the ages down the left hand side, we have four headings across the top. These are –

■ Development matters

■ Look, listen and note

■ Effective practice

■ Planning and resourcing.

What do these headings mean?

In the Practice Guidance Book, the information is clear –

Development matters 'identify the developing knowledge, skills, understanding and attitudes that children will need if they are to achieve the Early Learning Goals BY the end of the EYFS. It is important to note that children will not necessarily progress sequentially through the stages, since these do not represent age-related goals. By the end of the end of the EYFS, some children will have exceeded the goals, while others will be working towards some or all of them'.

Look, listen and note guides the practitioner in their 'observations of children which helps them to assess the progress children are making. Observations help practitioners to decide where children are in their learning and development and to plan what to do.

Effective practice guides practitioners towards ' forming a view of where each child is in their learning, where they need to go, and the most effective practice to support them

in getting there. The guidance on effective practice to support children's development is based on the EYFS principles and the examples given illustrate just some of the possibilities'.

Planning and resourcing reminds the practitioner that 'good planning is the key to making children's learning effective, exciting, varied and progressive. It enables practitioners to build up knowledge about how individual children learn and make progress. Plans should be flexible enough to adapt to circumstances'. If you refer to card –

3.4 Theme - Enabling Environments Commitment, Observation, Planning and Assessment.

you will find further guidance. This card helps you to make informed decisions about each child's progress, and suggests ways in which you can plan the next steps to meet their development and learning needs. This is your assessment of the child's learning.

KNOWLEDGE AND UNDERSTANDING OF THE WORLD 22 – 36 months (1 year 10 months - 3 years)

On pages 77, 79, 81, 83, 85, 87 of your Practice Guidance Book, you will find the 22-36 months section that relate to exploration and investigation, designing and making, ICT, time, place and communities.

What do you need to do next?

Read the sections for this age group that deal with

■ Development matters

■ Look, listen and note

■ Effective practice

■ Planning and resourcing.

Then consider the following for the young children –

Exploration and investigation

Do you –

■ recognise that when a child does such things a jumping in a puddle, they are engaging in an investigation?

Under this heading, you will find it useful to consider the additional information and guidance materials in Early Support. You will see references to Early Support on the cards in your EYFS pack. Under the heading of Knowledge and Understanding of the World for this age group, the Early Support programme suggests that you consider the following –

■ Talk about activities as children investigate things, for example, pouring water from one container to another or finding out what floats and what sinks. This helps children to understand what they are seeing and to learn the language they need to describe it

■ Encourage children to help you with everyday activities such as doing the washing up or cleaning. Give them a duster too. These are all 'games' to young children, as they explore their environment

■ Show children how a toy can be used, and then withdraw so they can try things out for themselves. Once they have mastered basic skills, show them how to take things further by introducing variation

■ Make up and share stories about the familiar sequences of events in a child's daily life. Use these to lead to discussion of past and future events

■ Interest children in books and stories for longer periods and allow them to observe the detail in more complex pictures. Choose books with colourful and realistic pictures that children can easily recognise

■ Show sensitivity to children when they want to do their own thing, but get involved in their play when they invite you. Your suggestions can help to extend the range of a child's play when you model actions, roles and imaginative ways of playing with familiar toys

■ Make junk models together. Use these and construction toys to help with imaginary games.

Design and making

Do you –

■ recognise that children's investigations may appear futile, but that a child may be on the brink of an amazing discovery for themselves?

ICT

Do you -

■ talk about ICT apparatus, what it does, what they can do with it and how to use it safely?

■ let children use the photocopier to copy their own pictures?

Time

Do you –

■ make a diary of photographs to record a special occasion?

■ Use the language of time such as 'yesterday', 'tomorrow' or 'next week'?

Place

Do you –

■ tell stories about places and journeys?

Communities

Do you –

■ encourage children to take on different roles during role play?

■ support children's friendships by talking to them about their characteristics, such as being kind, or fun to be with?

We have considered the 22 –36 months (1 year 10 months – 3 years) age group for the aspects of Knowledge and Understanding of the World. There is further information on the aspects for the other age groups within the EYFS pack and on the CD-ROM.

Physical Development

Let's look at the card from the pack, headed –

■ Learning and Development

■ Physical Development.

Under the heading on side one of the card, you will see the requirements of this area of learning.

The physical development of babies and young children must be encouraged through the provision of opportunities for them to be active and interactive and to improve their skills of co-ordination, control,

manipulation and movement. They must be supported in using all of their senses to learn about the world about them and to make connections between new information and what they already know. They must be supported in developing an understanding of the importance of physical activity and making healthy choices in relation to food.

At the bottom of side one of the card you will see the heading of physical development highlighted in red, to remind you of the area this card represents. The two boxes show the aspects of this area of learning, which are –

■ Movement and space

■ Health and bodily awareness

■ Using equipment and materials.

You need to familiarise your self with these aspect headings, and the statements in the second box, which explain what this area of learning means for children between birth and five years of age.

On side two of the card, the boxes show links to other cards in your packs – Positive Relationships and Enabling Environments.

(As with the other 6 cards under Learning and Development, you may have noticed that the **colours** for the two headings on side two of the card do not match the colours for Positive Relationships and Enabling

Environments. The green and purple colours are the wrong way round, but the content of the boxes is correct. This error in the colour has been noted by the Primary National Strategy and in the next print of the EYFS pack, the colours will be correct.)

So, how do you make the links to the areas of positive relationships and enabling environments?

Rather than just read the bullet points in the boxes, turn them into questions, to allow everyone in the setting to consider HOW they can effectively implement this area of learning and development –

1. How do we build children's confidence to take manageable risks in their play?

2. Do we motivate children to be active and help them to develop movement skills through praise, encouragement, games and appropriate guidance?

3. Do we value children's natural and spontaneous movements, through which they are finding out about their bodies and exploring sensations such as balance?

4. How much time do we give to supporting children's understanding of how exercise, eating, sleeping and hygiene promote good health?

5. Do we provide enough resources that will challenge and interest children - that can be used in a variety of ways, or to support specific skills?

6. Do we allow sufficient space, indoors and outdoors, to set up relevant activities for energetic play?

7. What opportunities do we offer to children with physical disabilities or motor impairments to develop their physical skills, working in partnership with relevant specialists?

8. Do we provide additional adult help, as necessary, to support individuals and to encourage increased independence in physical activities?

In the Learning and Development box on side two of the card, you will see ways in which you may help children under this area of learning. These points link into your Practice guidance books on pages 90-103. Let's look at this section of the book –

The information in this section is designed to help you observe, plan and assess your activities with children based on their individual development and needs.

On pages 92-103, you will see that there are four columns that represent the cycle of children's development in the area of physical development, for all the ages between 0-5 years. These ages are shown in months – refer back to page 8 of this book, to see the ages referred to in years, as well as months.

The sections **are not** intended to be all you need to consider – we know that children will do different things at different rates.

We must guard against using these sections as checklists.

On page 92 onwards of the Practice Guidance Book, we can see that, in addition to the ages down the left hand side, we have four headings across the top. These are –

■ Development matters

■ Look, listen and note

■ Effective practice

■ Planning and resourcing

What do these headings mean?

In the Practice Guidance Book, the information is clear –

Development matters 'identify the developing knowledge, skills, understanding and attitudes that children will need if they are to achieve the Early Learning Goals BY the end of the EYFS. It is important to note that children will not necessarily progress sequentially through the stages, since these do not represent age-related goals. By the end of the end of the EYFS, some children will have exceeded the goals, while others will be working towards some or all of them'.

Look, listen and note guides the practitioner in their 'observations of children which helps them to assess the progress children are making. Observations help practitioners to decide where children are in their learning and development and to plan what to do.

Effective practice guides practitioners towards ' forming a view of where

each child is in their learning, where they need to go, and the most effective practice to support them in getting there. The guidance on effective practice to support children's development is based on the EYFS principles and the examples given illustrate just some of the possibilities'.

Planning and resourcing reminds the practitioner that 'good planning is the key to making children's learning effective, exciting, varied and progressive. It enables practitioners to build up knowledge about how individual children learn and make progress. Plans should be flexible enough to adapt to circumstances'. If you refer to card –

3.5 Theme - Enabling Environments Commitment, Observation, Planning and Assessment.

you will find further guidance. This card helps you to make informed decisions about each child's progress, and suggests ways in which you can plan the next steps to meet their development and learning needs. This is your assessment of the child's learning.

PHYSICAL DEVELOPMENT 30 – 50 months (2 years 6 months – 4 years 2 months)

On pages 94, 95, 99, 102, of your Practice Guidance Book, you will find the 30 - 50 months section that relate to movement and space, health and bodily awareness and using equipment and materials.

What do you need to do next?

Read the sections for this age group that deal with

■ Development matters

■ Look, listen and note

■ Effective practice

■ Planning and resourcing.

Then consider the following for the young children –

Movement and space

Do you –

■ teach skills which will help children to keep themselves safe, for example, responding rapidly to signals including visual signs and notes of music?

- encourage children to move with controlled effort, and use associated vocabulary such as 'strong', 'firm', 'gentle', 'heavy', 'stretch', 'reach', 'tense' and 'floppy'?

- use music to create moods and talk about how people move when they are sad, happy or cross?

- lead imaginative movement sessions based on children's current interests such as space travel, zoo animals or shadows?

- motivate children to be active through games such as follow the leader?

- talk about why children should take care when moving freely, and help them to remember some simple rules to remind them how to move about without endangering themselves or others?

- praise children's efforts when they consider others or work together in tasks?

- encourage children to persevere through praise, guidance or instruction when success is not immediate?

Under this heading, you will find it useful to consider the additional information and guidance materials in Early Support. You will see references to Early Support on the cards in your EYFS pack. Under the heading of Movement and Space for this age group, the Early Support programme suggests that you consider the following:

- use singing, music and movement games to reinforce understanding of different parts of the body and body positions. Try games such as 'head shoulder, knees and toes'

- begin to use introduce the ideas of left and right. You may consider using a sticker to mark one hand

- demonstrate how to move backwards and practise by dancing. An example of this would be the 'hokey kokey'

- encourage children to jump off low steps into your arms and then later, onto the floor. At this stage,

children may enjoy learning how to walk along low walls or benches and jumping off at the end. Give support to begin with, but balance will improve with practice

- play games that involve reaching up high to encourage children to stand on their toes. Challenge children to walk as quietly as possible on crinkly paper, leaves or pebbles. This also helps children to walk on tiptoe. You may need to hold hands initially

- Demonstrate how to push the pedals on a tricycle and encourage children to do this independently.

Health and bodily awareness

Do you –

- talk to the children about why you encourage them to rest when they are tired or why they need to wear wellington boots when it is muddy outside?

- create opportunities for moving towards independence, for example, have hand washing facilities safely within reach, and support children in making healthy choices about the food they eat?

- encourage children to notice the changes in their bodies after exercise, such as their heart beating faster?

Using equipment and materials

Do you –

- teach children they skills they need to use equipment safely, for example, cutting with scissors?

- check children's clothing for safety, for example, checking that toggles on coats and hoods cannot get tangled in tricycle wheels?

- introduce the vocabulary of direction?

Under this heading, you will find it useful to consider the additional information and guidance materials in Early Support. You will see references to Early Support on the cards in your EYFS pack. Under the heading of Movement and Space for this age group, the Early Support programme suggests that you consider the following –

- match pictures with colours and play with pictures and objects that can be sorted into two groups by size, shape, or colour. Socks (big ones for adults and small ones for children) or cutlery work well.

- help children to develop their manual dexterity by showing them how to unwrap small objects covered in paper. Help them to use scissors too.

- encourage children to enjoy scribbling using thick pens and paintbrushes. Some children will enjoy copying a line across or up and down a sheet of paper or copying a large circle.

- show children how to make marks in dough and feel the marks they have made.

We have considered the 30 –50 months (2 years 6 months – 4 years 2 months) age group for the aspects of Physical Development. There is further information on the aspects for the other age groups within the EYFS pack and on the CD-ROM.

CREATIVE DEVELOPMENT

Let's look at the card from the pack, headed –

- Learning and Development

- Creative Development.

Under the heading on side one of the card, you will see the requirements of this area of learning.

Children's creativity must be extended by the provision of support for their curiosity, exploration and play. They must be provided with opportunities to explore and share their thoughts, ideas and feelings, for example, through a variety of art, music, movement, dance, imaginative and role play activities, mathematics, and design and technology.

At the bottom of side one of the card you will see the heading of creative development highlighted in red, to remind you of the area this card represents. The two boxes show the aspects of this area of learning, which are –

- Being creative – responding to experiences, expressing and communicating ideas.

■ Exploring media and materials.

■ Creating music an dance.

■ Developing imagination and imaginative play.

You need to familiarise your self with these aspect headings, and the statements in the second box, which explain what this area of learning means for children between birth and five years of age.

On side two of the card, the boxes show links to other cards in your packs – Positive Relationships and Enabling Environments.

(As with the other 6 cards under Learning and Development, you may have noticed that the **colours** for the two headings on side two of the card do not match the colours for Positive Relationships and Enabling Environments. The green and purple colours are the wrong way round, but the content of the boxes is correct. This error in the colour has been noted by the Primary National Strategy and in the next print of the EYFS pack, the colours will be correct.)

So, how do you make the links to the areas of positive relationships and enabling environments?

Rather than just read the bullet points in the boxes, turn them into questions, to allow everyone in the setting to consider HOW they can effectively implement this area of learning and development –

1. How do we ensure that children feel secure enough to 'have a go', learn new things and be adventurous?

2. Do we value what children can do and children's own ideas rather than expecting them to reproduce someone else's picture, dance or model, for example?

3. Do we offer opportunities for children to work alongside artists and other creative adults so that they see at first hand different ways of expressing and communicating ideas and different responses to media and materials?

4. Do we accommodate children's specific religious or cultural beliefs relating to particular forms of art or methods of representation?

5. Do we provide a stimulating environment in which creativity, originality and expressiveness are valued?

6. Do we include resources from a variety of cultures to stimulate new ideas and different ways of thinking?

7. Do we offer opportunities for children with visual impairment to access and have physical contact with artefacts and materials?

8. Do we provide opportunities for children with hearing impairment to experience sound through physical contact with instruments and other sources of sound?

9. How do we encourage children who cannot communicate by voice to respond to music in different ways, such as gestures?

In the Learning and Development box on side two of the card, you will see ways in which you may help children under this area of learning. These points link into your Practice guidance books on pages 104-114. Let's look at this section of the book –

The information in this section is designed to help you observe, plan and assess your activities with children based on their individual development and needs.

On pages 106-114, you will see that there are four columns that represent the cycle of children's development in the area of creative development, for all the ages between 0-5 years. These ages are shown in months – refer back to page 8 of this book, to see the ages referred to in years, as well as months.

The sections **are not** intended to be all you need to consider – we know that children will do different things at different rates.

We must guard against using these sections as checklists.

On page 106 onwards of the Practice Guidance Book, we can see that, in addition to the ages down the left hand side, we have four headings across the top. These are –

■ Development matters

■ Look, listen and note

■ Effective practice

■ Planning and resourcing.

What do these headings mean?

In the Practice Guidance Book, the information is clear –

Development matters 'identify the developing knowledge, skills, understanding and attitudes that children will need if they are to achieve the Early Learning Goals BY the end of the EYFS. It is important to note that children will not necessarily progress sequentially through the stages, since these do not represent age-related goals. By the end of the end of the EYFS, some children will have exceeded the goals, while others will be working towards some or all of them'.

Look, listen and note guides the practitioner in their 'observations of children which helps them to assess the progress children are making. Observations help practitioners to decide where children are in their learning and development and to plan what to do.

Effective practice guides practitioners towards ' forming a view of where each child is in their learning, where they need to go, and the most effective practice to support them in getting there. The guidance on effective practice to support children's development is based on the EYFS principles and the examples given illustrate just some of the possibilities'.

Planning and resourcing reminds the practitioner that 'good planning is the key to making children's learning effective, exciting, varied and progressive. It enables practitioners to build up knowledge about how individual children learn and make progress. Plans should be flexible enough to adapt to circumstances'. If you refer to card –

3.6 Theme - Enabling Environments Commitment, Observation, Planning and Assessment.

you will find further guidance. This card helps you to make informed decisions about each child's progress, and suggests ways in which you can plan the next steps to meet their development and learning needs. This is your assessment of the child's learning.

CREATIVE DEVELOPMENT 40 – 60 +months (3 years 4 months - 5 + years)

On pages 107, 110, 112, 114, of your Practice Guidance Book, you will find the 40-60 + months section that relate to being creative – responding to experiences, expressing and communicating ideas, exploring media and materials, creating music and dance, and developing imagination and imaginative play.

What do you need to do next?

Read the sections for this age group that deal with

■ Development matters

■ Look, listen and note

■ Effective practice

■ Planning and resourcing.

Then consider the following for the young children –

Being creative – responding to experiences, expressing and communicating ideas

Do you –

■ support children in expressing opinions and produce language such as 'like', dislike', 'prefer', 'disagree'?

■ alert yourselves to children's changing interest and the way in which they respond to experiences differently when they are in a happy, sad or reflective mood?

Exploring media and materials

Do you –

■ help children to gain confidence in their own ways of representing ideas?

■ talk to children about ways of finding out what they can do with different media and what happens when they put different things together such as sand, paint and sawdust?

■ help children to develop a problem-solving approach to overcome hindrances as they explore possibilities those media combinations present? Offer

advice and additional resources as appropriate

■ alert children to changes in properties of media as they are transformed through becoming wet, dry, flaky or fixed? Talk about what is happening, helping them to think about 'cause and affect'.

Creating music and dance

Do you –

■ support children's developing understanding of the ways in which paintings, pictures and music and dance can express different ideas, thoughts and feelings?

■ encourage discussion about the beauty of nature and people's responsibility to care for it? Help children to support other children and offer another viewpoint.

Developing imagination and imaginative play

Do you –

■ make links between imaginative play and children's own ability to handle narrative?

■ carefully support children who are less confident?

■ introduce descriptive language to support children, for example, 'rustle' and 'shuffle'?

We have considered the 40 –60 + months (3 years 4 months – 5 + years) age group for the aspects of Creative Development. There is further information on the aspects for the other age groups within the EYFS pack and on the CD-ROM.

The Stepping Stones and the Early Learning Goals

The summative assessment at the end of the EYFS is the EYFS Profile based on the early learning goals for each area of learning and development. It is therefore important that ALL practitioners understand how the work they are doing with the youngest babies and children contributes in the long term to the early learning goals. The stepping stones from the Curriculum Guidance for the Foundation Stage are still present in the areas of Learning and Development in the columns of 'Development Matters'.

In the Practice Guidance book, which sets the standards for learning, development and care of under 5's, the text under the headings of 'development matters', look, listen and note', 'effective practice', and planning and resourcing', is taken mainly from the Birth – Three Framework, the Curriculum Guidance for the Foundation Stage and the National Standards for Under 8's Day care and Childminding – familiar to all. Some of the Standards, for example, those to do with the physical environment, are in the registration and Welfare Requirements. Others, for example, relating to care, learning and play, have become a part of the learning and development requirements. The message is clear – this document is not 'new'. It enables all practitioners to work with children from birth – five year in a seamless way – meeting the care and educational needs of all.

The EYFS scales, points 1-3, within the Profile will still be assessed using the same statements originally derived from the stepping stones as they cover important knowledge and skills which are still included in the EYFS. Scale points 4-8 are based on the early learning goals, which are still there in the EYFS. Scale point 9 continues to be a statement of achievement beyond the early learning goals.

Let's use one area of learning and development as an example –

Knowledge and Understanding of the World

In the Practice Guidance book, under each area of learning, the final section, leading on from the age group of 40-60 months, shows the Early Learning Goals for that area. For our example, you will find the information on page 86.

The Early Learning Goals for this area are –

■ Observe, find out about and identify features in the place they live and the natural world

■ Find out about their environment, and talk about those features they like and dislike.

Within the EYFS profile

1. Shows curiosity and interest by exploring surroundings

2. Observes, selects and manipulates objects and materials. Identifies simple features and significant personal events

3. Identifies obvious similarities and differences when exploring and observing. Constructs in a purposeful way, using simple tools and techniques.

These first three points describe a child who is still progressing towards the achievements described in the Early Learning Goals for Knowledge and Understanding of the World. Most children will achieve all three of these points before they achieve any of the early learning goals.

4. Investigates places, objects, materials and living things by using all the senses as appropriate. Identifies some features and talks about those features he/she dislikes

5. Asks questions about why things happen and how things work. Looks closely at similarities, differences, patterns and change

6. Finds out about past and present events in own life, and in those of family members and other people he/she knows. Begins to know about own culture and beliefs and those of other people

7. Finds out about and identifies the uses of everyday technology and uses information and communication technology and programmable toys to support his/her learning

8. Builds and constructs with a wide range of objects, selecting appropriate resources, tools and techniques and adapting his/her work where necessary.

These five points are drawn from the early learning goals themselves. These are presented in approximate order of difficulty, according to evidence from trials. Remember that each child's learning is achieved at their own pace, and therefore a child may achieve a later point without having achieved some of the earlier points.

9. Communicates simple planning for investigations and constructions and makes simple records and evaluations of his/her work. Identifies and names key features and properties, sometimes linking different experiences, observations and events. Begins to explore what it means to belong to a variety of groups and communities.

This last point describes a child who has achieved all the points from 1-8 as described above for Knowledge and Understanding of the World. The child has developed further both in breadth and depth, and is working consistently beyond the level of the early learning goal.

The scales of assessment for all areas of learning can be found on pages 44 – 48 of the Statutory Framework book.

Reception class teachers have asked about the Primary Frameworks for Literacy and Mathematics – how are these represented with the EYFS? At this time, the early learning goals remain the outcomes that children in reception classes are working towards. The links between the Frameworks and the EYFS are shown by the Early Learning goals

being highlighted in the Frameworks – effective practice for all practitioners can be found in the EYFS document. The links to Key Stage 1 are strong.

Excellence and Enjoyment; a Strategy for Primary Schools 'affirms a vision for primary education that provides opportunities for all children to succeed through a commitment to high standards and excellence within an exciting, engaging, broad and rich curriculum. There should be little difficulty in making links between EYFS and Key Stage 1'. This document can be obtained from the DfES publications 0845 6022260.

Excellence and Enjoyment; Learning and Teaching in the Primary Years is also available from the DfES publications line. 'It is a set of development materials, which help practitioners make links. The booklets and video provide in the pack include examples of effective practice in working with 3-5 year olds, as well as with older children, and show where each of the key aspects of learning are embedded in the areas of learning and the programme of study for Key Stage 1 and Key Stage 2. The key aspects of learning provide a framework for continuing the broad and balanced approach to the EYFS'. The aspects of effective learning are empathy, motivation, managing feelings, social skills, and communication. Aspects of cognition are reasoning, evaluation, creativity, enquiry, problem solving and information processing.

The pack, **Continuing the Learning Journey**, was sent to every primary school in 2005. This document 'demonstrates how the EYFS Profile should be used as an effective transfer document for children, so that their learning and development across the whole curriculum is maintained'.

The Requirements of the Assessment Arrangements are

■ that providers must ensure that each child is assessed by a practitioner within their final year of the EYFS

■ practitioners must use the 13 scales and have regard to the scales point as set out on pages 44-48 of the Statutory Booklet

■ the assessment must be completed in the final term of the year in which the child reaches the age of five

years and no later than the 30th June in that term

■ providers must permit the relevant local authority to enter the premises at all reasonable times in order to observe the implementation of the arrangements for the completion of the EYFS Profile

■ providers must permit the relevant local authority to examine and take copies of documents and other articles relating to the EYFS Profile and assessments

■ providers must take part in all reasonable moderation activities as specified by their local authority

■ providers must provide the relevant local authority with such information relating to the EYFS Profile and assessment as they may reasonably request

■ within the final term of the EYFS providers must provide the parent of a child in relation to whom the EYFS Profile has been completed –

1. A written summary reporting the child's progress against the early learning goals and the assessment scales

2. Where the parent requests it, a copy of the EYFS Profile

3. Details of the arrangements under which the EYFS Profile and its results may be discussed between a practitioner and the parent, giving a reasonable opportunity for the parent to discuss the EYFS Profile and its results with that practitioner

4. Where a child moves to a new provider during the academic year, the provider should send the following information to the new provider within 15 days of a request from the new provider –

   a) any EYFS Profile data recorded by the EYFS provider

   b) the provider's assessment made in respect of the child

   c) if no EYFS Profile of the child has been recorded by the EYFS provider, the reason why the assessment has not been carried out.

Providers may use the EYFS optional scales booklet (published by the Qualifications and Curriculum Authority, QCA) or their own record keeping system. Children with special educational needs may be working below the level of the scales and require an alternative approach to assessment. In these cases, providers may use the assessment systems of their local authority or other systems according to the needs of the children. Regulations made under Section 99 of the Childcare Act 2006 require early years providers to provide information about the assessments they carry out, to local authorities, who have a duty to return this data to the DfES.

The Welfare Requirements

Children learn best when they are healthy, safe and secure, when their individual needs are met and when they have positive relationships with the adults caring for them. The welfare requirements are designed to support providers in creating settings which are welcoming, safe and stimulating, and where children are able to enjoy learning through play, to grow in confidence and to fulfil their potential.

The Welfare Requirements have been drawn together from elements of the National Standards for Under 8's Daycare and Childminding. The EYFS sets out the legal requirements that all providers must meet, regardless of type, size or funding of the setting. The Practice Guidance book and supporting resources provide information and advice designed to help practitioners meet these legal requirements in a way that reflects the needs of the individual children in their care and is appropriate to their setting.

It is essential that children are provided with safe and secure environments in which to interact and explore rich and diverse learning and development opportunities. Providers need to ensure that, as well as conducting a formal risk assessment, they constantly reappraise both the environments and activities to which children are being exposed and make necessary adjustments to secure their safety at all times.

Schools will not be required to have separate policies for the EYFS provided that the requirements are met through their policies, which cover children of statutory school age.

It is an offence to fail to comply with some of the welfare requirements. It is an offence for a provider to –

1. fail to notify Ofsted of certain events, which are set out in the relevant welfare requirements

2. give corporal punishment to a child, as set out under behaviour management on page 28 in the Statutory Framework book.

Where Ofsted considers that a provider has failed to comply with any of the welfare requirements, they may give notice to the provider setting out –

1. in what respect the provider has failed to comply with the requirements

2. what action the provider should take to comply

3. the period within which the provider should take that action. It is an offence for a provider to fail to comply with such a notice.

We need to consider the general legal requirements and the detail in the specific legal requirements. Both the general and specific legal requirements have the force of regulations and therefore must be complied with by all early years providers. Providers must also have regard to the statutory guidance – we need to consider how you can take the guidance into account when you seek to fulfil the general and specific requirements.

So, what are the Welfare Requirements?

- Safeguarding and promoting children's welfare

- Suitable people

- Suitable premises, environment and equipment

- Organisation

- Documentation.

Ofsted will base the inspections from September 2008 on whether a provider has met the general and specific requirements, and can show that they have given regard to the statutory guidance.

Let's look at each of the welfare requirements. In the Statutory Framework book, from pages 22-40, you will see the legal and specific requirements shown for each of the five welfare requirements, and the statutory guidance linked to the requirements. In the Practice Guidance book, in section 3, pages 14-18, you will find additional information on how you may meet the requirements, and how the welfare requirements link to the overall EYFS document.

Safeguarding and promoting children's welfare

The general requirements are –

- The provider must take the necessary steps to safeguard and promote the welfare of children (specific requirements 1-5)

- The provider must promote the good health of children, take necessary steps to prevent the spread of infection, and take appropriate action when children are ill (specific requirements 6–9)

- Children's behaviour must be managed effectively and in a manner appropriate for their stage of development and particular individual needs (specific requirements 10).

The cards that broadly link to the general requirements 1-5 are A Unique Child card 1.4 (Health and well-being) and Positive Relationships 2.4 (Key person).

1. Safeguarding

2. Information and complaints

3. Premises and security

4. Outings

5. Equality of opportunity

6. Medicines

7. Illnesses and injuries

8. Food and drink

9. Smoking

10. Behaviour management

Let's look at each one of the specific requirements –

1. Safeguarding

The specific requirements broadly links to cards 1.3 and 1.4, which are –

- A Unique Child (Keeping Safe) and A Unique Child (Health and Well being).

Remember that both the general and specific legal requirements have the force of regulations and therefore must be complied with by all early years providers.

You will see that some specific legal requirements have links to the EYFS through the cards and the areas of learning. You may find it helpful as we consider 'safeguarding', to have the cards to refer to as well as Practice Guidance book.

What must you do for the specific requirements?

1. Ensure that you have an effective Safeguarding policy and procedure in place

2. Inform Ofsted without delay of any allegations of serious harm or abuse by any person living, working or looking after the children at the premises. Providers must also inform the Local Safeguarding Children Board without delay, of allegations of abuse. Ensure that concerns are kept confidential

3. Ensure that all members of staff are aware of the procedures that will be followed in the event of an allegation being made against a member of staff.

4. Ensure that you have a named designated person in your setting to take the lead in implementing your safeguarding policy and procedure.

The Statutory guidance (to which you must give regard) is helpful –

- Consider how, through training, all staff can become familiar with your policy and procedure so that they are clear about their responsibilities in safeguarding and protecting child, and understand what will happen in the event of an allegation being made against any member of staff. Your written policy and procedure should be in line with the Local Safeguarding Children Board guidance – contact your local authority for training opportunities for this area of the welfare requirements

- Training will ensure that your staff will be able to respond appropriately to concerns they may have about a child.

Staff should be able to respond appropriately to –

a) significant changes in children's behaviour. Refer to children aged 22-36 months, personal, social and emotional development; look listen and note and refer to children aged 22-36 months, personal, social and emotional development; planning and resourcing

b) deterioration in their general well-being

c) unexplained bruising, marks or signs of possible abuse

d) neglect

e) the comments children make which give cause for concern. Refer to children aged 22-36 months, personal, social and emotional development; look listen and note and refer to children aged 30-50 months, knowledge and understanding of the world; effective practice.

It is very easy to say that the welfare, safety and protection of all children is of paramount importance, but how do you achieve this? If we think about children being vulnerable and in need of adult protection, we have a starting point. Children do not always recognise dangers, and therefore it is the adult's responsibility to help them to understand when they may be facing a dangerous situation, and guide them towards thinking of their own safety. This seems simple enough if we are considering, for example, water safety, or the use of a climbing frame. Children will come to understand that they may get injured in certain situations, so it is best for them to think about what they are doing to make sure that they can play safely.

The welfare of children must be your primary consideration, not just with respect to alerting them to safety issues in their play, but to safety in respect of their whole being. This means that you need to be aware of child protection issues. Training in this sensitive area is necessary for staff working in settings and also for childminders, so that everyone will fully understand their responsibilities to the children in their care.

You should have a copy of your Local Safeguarding Children Board procedures – this is your starting point for what you need to write in your policy and procedures. The information is not just for day care provision, but for all people who work in any capacity with children. The book will explain in detail about the law, and how this affect you in you work with young children. It explains what the term 'abuse' means. It is also clear that you have a duty to protect the children in your care from abuse.

The wording of your policy for protecting children is important. You could consider this in the following way –

Safeguarding and Protecting Children

The safety and well-being of your children is our primary responsibility. If we have any concerns about your child, we will speak to you in the first instance, and hope that you will approach your key person if you have any concerns about your child.

This statement will tell parents that nothing matters more than the welfare of their child, and you would not hesitate to speak to the parents about any concerns you may have. This should be a reassurance to the parents.

Our staff have attended training in child protection issues, and understand their responsibilities in safeguarding children.

This statement will tell parents that the staff have the knowledge necessary to address any issues relating to the welfare of children. This too should be a reassurance to the parents, who will appreciate you being alert to these matters.

We adhere to the procedures set out in the Local Safeguarding Children Board Procedure Book. It is our duty to report any concern we may have regarding the children in our care. This is primarily to safeguard the children. *Parents will be clear about your role in safeguarding their children.*

We have a designated member of staff who is our liaison person for child protection. The designated person is able to contact the local child protection co-ordinator within Social Services for advice on child protection matters. If a member of staff has a concern about a child, the designated member of staff will be informed. A decision about how to inform you of our concerns will be made with minimum people involved. We work within the bounds of confidentiality. *Parents will be clear that you have a duty to protect children, and would contact the child protection co-ordinator for advice if necessary.*

Your main concern is for the welfare of the children in your setting. The staff should all be aware of their responsibility in this area, but should also be aware of the importance of protecting themselves against allegations of abuse. In a group setting, it is unlikely that a member of staff would be alone for more than a couple of minutes with a child, but this may happen if, for example, a child

had an accident, and needed to be taken to the toilet area to be changed. The member of staff could protect themselves by –

1. Informing other staff of the situation, and state that the child is about to be taken to the toilet area to be changed

2. If possible, remain in sight of other adults

3. Deal as quickly as possible with the child, and then return to the main group

4. Tell another member of staff what you have done, and then advise the parent of the situation when the child is collected.

In this way, you have cared appropriately for the child, made sure that someone knows what you were doing, and then you have advised the parents at the end of the day/session.

2. Information and complaints

The specific requirements broadly links to cards 1.1 and 1.3, which are –

■ A Unique Child (Child Development) and A Unique Child (Keeping Safe).

Remember that both the general and specific legal requirements have the force of regulations and therefore must be complied with by all early years providers.

What must you do for the specific requirements?

1. Providers are expected to engage with parents on all matters relating their child's welfare and well being. Look on page 23 of the Statutory Guidance book. You will a checklist of the specific legal requirements

2. Look at this information with the staff in your setting. Do all of the 13 bullet points apply to your setting?

Bullet point 4 (food and drinks provided for the children) – refer to children aged between 22-26 months, physical development; planning and resourcing.

Bullet point 11 (the child's special dietary requirements, preferences or food allergies the child may have) – refer to children aged between birth – 11 months, physical development; planning and resourcing.

Look at the 5 statements underneath the bullet points – they all include 'You must…' Everyone needs to be aware of what MUST be in place.

The Statutory guidance (to which you must give regard) is helpful –

Think about HOW you do the following –

■ maintain a regular two-way flow of information with parents and between providers (for example, where a childminder regularly collects a child from a nursery)?

■ ensure that all staff are aware of the need to maintain and confidentiality?

■ allow parents free access to developmental records about their children and, when requested, include comments from parents into children's records?

■ keep and store, confidentially, records of complaints for at least three years?

Remember that a written request must be made for personal files on the children and providers must take into account and comply with data protection rules when disclosing records that refer to third parties.

3. Premises and security

Remember that both the general and specific legal requirements have the force of regulations and therefore must be complied with by all early years providers.

You will see that some specific legal requirements have links to the EYFS through the cards and the areas of learning. You may find it helpful as we consider 'safeguarding', to have the cards to refer to as well as Practice Guidance book.

What must you do for the specific requirements?

1. The premises, both indoors and outside, must be safe and secure

2. Providers must notify Ofsted of any change to the facilities to be used fore care that may affect the space and level of care available to the children. Any provider who, reasonable excuse, fails to comply with this requirement, commits an offence

3. Providers must only release children into the care of individuals named

by the parent. Refer to children aged between 8-20 months, personal, social and emotional development; planning and resourcing

4. Providers must ensure that children do not leave the premises unsupervised

5. Providers must take steps to prevent intruders entering the premises.

The Statutory guidance (to which you must give regard) is helpful –

Look on page 24 of the Statutory Guidance book. You will find a checklist of the specific legal requirements.

Look at this information with the staff in your setting. Do all of the 7 bullet points apply to your setting?

■ What security systems do you have in place, to ensure the safety of all the children?

■ Are all staff aware of the whereabouts of other people on the premises and of any other users on the premises, if this applies to you setting? Refer to children aged 30-50 months, personal, social and emotional development; effective practice

■ What information do make available about your systems of security, for example, posters? Refer to children aged 22-36 months, physical development; planning and resourcing

■ What systems do you have in place for identifying visitors, recording their names, the purpose of their visit, and recording of arrival and departure times? Refer to children aged 16-26 months, knowledge and understanding of the world; planning and resourcing, and refer to children aged 40-60 months, knowledge and understanding of the world; effective practice

■ Do you have a system for recording the arrivals and departures of staff, children and parents too?

■ Do you obtain permission (preferably in writing) from parents when children are to be picked up by another adult?

4. Outings

Remember that both the general and specific legal requirements have the force of regulations and therefore must be complied with by all early years providers.

You will see that some specific legal requirements have links to the EYFS through the cards and the areas of learning. You may find it helpful as we consider 'safeguarding', to have the cards to refer to as well as Practice Guidance book.

What must you do for the specific requirements?

1. Children must be kept safe whilst on outings. Refer to children aged 30-50 months, knowledge and understanding

of the world; effective practice. Refer to children aged 30-50 months, knowledge and understanding of the world; planning and resourcing

2. For each outing, providers must carry out a full risk assessment, which includes an assessment of required adult:child ratios. This assessment must take account of the nature of the outing. Consideration must be given as to whether it is appropriate to exceed the normal ratio requirements.

The Statutory guidance (to which you must give regard) is helpful –

Think about HOW you do the following –

■ Obtain the written parental permission for all children to take part in outings?

■ Ensure that staff take essential records and equipment on outings, such as contact numbers for the parents, first aid kit with individual medication as necessary, a mobile phone?

■ Record details about the vehicles in which children may be transported, including insurance and a list of named drivers?

5. Equality of opportunities

Remember that both the general and specific legal requirements have the force of regulations and therefore must be complied with by all early years providers.

You will see that some specific legal requirements have links to the EYFS through the cards and the areas of learning. You may find it helpful to have the cards to refer to as well as Practice Guidance book.

What must you do for the specific requirements?

1. All providers must have and implement an effective policy about ensuring equality of opportunities and for supporting children with difficulties and disabilities. Refer to children aged 40–60+ months, physical development; effective practice. Refer to babies aged birth – 11 months, physical development; effective practice. Refer to children aged 30-50 months, physical development; planning and resourcing

2. All providers in receipt of Government funding, must have regard to the SEN Code of Practice.

Look on page 25 of the Statutory Guidance book. You will see a checklist of what your policy on equality of opportunity should include.

Look at this information with the staff in your setting. Do all of the 9 bullet points apply to your setting? This may be training need for staff in your setting.

In particular, bullet point 2, 'information about how all children, including those who are disabled or have special educational needs, will be included, valued and supported, and how reasonable adjustments will be made for them' Refer to children aged –

■ 40-60+ months, creative development; planning and resourcing

■ 8-20 months, personal, social and emotional development; planning and resourcing

■ 16-26 months, personal, social and emotional development; planning and resourcing

■ 16-26 months, personal, social and emotional development; planning and resourcing

■ 40-60+ months, personal, social and emotional development; effective practice

■ 40-60+ months, personal, social and emotional development; planning and resourcing

■ birth-11 months, personal, social and emotional development; effective practice

■ 8-20 months, communication, language and literacy; effective practice

■ birth-11 months, communication, language and literacy; effective practice

■ 16-26 months, communication language and literacy; effective practice.

In particular, bullet point 7 'information about how the provision will promote and value diversity and differences'. Refer to children aged 16-26 months, personal social and emotional development; effective practice, and refer to children aged 16-26 months,

personal, social and emotional development; planning and resourcing.

In particular, bullet point 8 'information about how inappropriate attitudes and practices will be challenged' Refer to children aged 40-60+ months, knowledge and understanding of the world; effective practice

We need to think about what the term 'equal opportunities' means. If you were to ask this question, many would reply 'Well, it means to treat everyone the same'. This response is understandable – if you treat everyone in the same way, you are not treating anyone differently, and this must be fair. Or is it?

Let's consider what effect this would have on the children in your care. If you were to treat children in exactly the same way, that is, to give the same toys to all the children, the same food, and expect the same level of work from them, what difficulties could there be for the children?

The answer lies in the word 'same'. You need to think of each child as an individual, not as a part of a group that is given the 'same' as everyone else.

You need to consider **choice** of the range of toys and play materials you have in your setting.

You need to consider food **preferences/allergies** when you are putting together your menus.

You need to consider each child in terms of their **age/developmental** stage when planning your curriculum or programme.

'Equal opportunities' needs to be considered for the children, the staff and the parents. In this way, you will be able to show how you respect everyone, regardless of their circumstances.

Your policies and procedures are a clear statement of how you will approach your care of the care of the children in your setting. The key to a well-worded policy on equal opportunity is how you explain what you mean by 'treating all children according to their individual needs'.

Explain – that you recognise that all children develop at their own pace, and that your curriculum has been planned to enable all children to develop to their potential.

Explain – that you recognise the importance of involving parents in the forming of the policy document.

Explain – that you intend to develop in the children a real sense of belonging in the community/society, recognising cultural differences, and celebrating them

Explain – that you are committed to promoting our diverse society in a positive way.

Explain – that you encourage your staff to attend training on issues relating to inclusion, to give them an even greater understanding of the issues they face in caring for young children in today's world.

Explain – how you will put the policy into practice. This will mean giving an explanation of your procedures that staff follow, to implement the written policy.

REMEMBER - the families you work with may not speak or understand English. In most settings, policies and procedures are written in English. It can be very costly to have all your documents written in other languages, so how can you deal with this? It may be that you are working in an area where there are many families who, for example, speak Urdu. It may seem sensible to arrange for your documents to be written in Urdu also for that community. But what about the one child who is, for example, Chinese? These are difficulties that some settings face, and then there is an expectation that an equal opportunities policy to include everyone will be produced! The best way to deal with this is to think practically about the issues.

Do you have a welcome poster, that is displayed in the entrance, to offer a greeting to everyone, regardless of the language barriers?

Do you have a contact within your local education service that could put you in contact with an interpreter, for the families that will have difficulties in communicating with the staff?

Do the staff feel confident in challenging inappropriate comments?

Does your book selection reflect our diverse society?

Do your pictures and posters show positive images of male and female roles, people of different colours and abilities etc.?

All of these things, and others that you may have already put in place, will demonstrate how you think of each family and child as individual, recognising their needs, and promoting their language/cultural differences in a positive way. It must be stressed that equal opportunities is not just about the colour of skin – there are wider issues for everyone to consider –

■ Language

■ Ability

■ Age

■ Cultures and beliefs.

Encourage your staff to attend any training that will enable them to learn about other people's cultures and beliefs.

We need to think about those people who are regularly discriminated against in today's society. They may include older people, people with white or black skin colour, large people, small people, individuals with a physical disability, those for whom English is a second language, gifted people, gay and lesbian people – the list goes on, because at some time in everyone's life, there is a feeling that 'I do not get a fair chance in society. This is because I am..........'. (perhaps one of the listed). You may wonder 'Who is normal, then?' The answer to this question is not easy. We all, at some stage, are not satisfied with, for example, our appearance, work efforts, communication skills etc. To then hear unkind comments about this is not good for our feelings, so imagine how a child may feel in a similar situation. Each child needs to feel that they are a part of your setting – a part of their peer group – a part of the local community.

Children should be encouraged to share experiences within the group – introduce a news time, so that all children can share their special news with everyone, for example, what they did at the weekend, news about a baby brother or sister being born, information about their pets etc. This will build children's self esteem, and encourage them to explore their feelings. A wall chart showing faces with different expressions to represent happy, sad, cross, unsure etc. is an excellent way of helping children to talk about their feelings in a non- threatening way.

Your play resources – what is available for each child to have access to? Do you consider providing a wide range range of toys and play materials for boys and girls, reflecting our multicultural society, books and jigsaws, and role play opportunities, exploiting the home corner in a variety of ways? Are all play materials available to all the children, regardless of age, gender, ability? Importantly, do your play activities enable children to gain some understanding of other people's views?

Many settings state that they 'value diversity'. If this is written into your policy, is there an understanding of what the term means? There is no point in writing policies that the staff cannot explain. The Oxford Dictionary helps us with 'valuing diversity' –

■ value – usefulness, importance

■ diversity – variety.

These explanations help us to think about the various backgrounds, abilities, cultures, faiths, languages etc. of the families we work with in our society. For staff to recognise the importance of respect for other people's way of life, and not be judgmental about those choices, is a key factor in how this welfare requirement can be met in your setting.

Let's look back to what the general requirements are –

■ The provider must take the necessary steps to safeguard and promote the welfare of children (specific requirements 1-5)

■ The provider must promote the good health of children, take necessary steps to prevent the spread of infection, and take appropriate action when children are ill (specific requirements 6-9)

■ Children's behaviour must be managed effectively and in a manner appropriate for their stage of development and particular individual needs (specific requirements 10).

We have looked at the specific requirements 1-5.

The card that broadly links to the general requirements 6-9 are A Unique Child card 1.4 (Health and well-being)

Remember that both the general and specific legal requirements have the force of regulations and therefore must be complied with by all early years providers.

You will see that some specific legal requirements have links to the EYFS through the cards and the areas of learning. You may find it helpful to have the cards to refer to as well as Practice Guidance book.

6. Medicines

Remember that both the general and specific legal requirements have the force of regulations and therefore must be complied with by all early years providers.

What must you do for the specific requirements?

1. Providers must implement an effective policy on administering medicines. The policy must include effective management systems to support individual children with medical needs

2. Providers must keep written records of all prescribed medicines administered to children, and inform parents

3. Providers must obtain prior written permission for each and every medicine from parents before any medication is given.

The Statutory guidance (to which you must give regard) is helpful –

Look on page 26 of the Statutory guidance book. You will find 4 points to consider. Think about how you –

1. Ensure that you have sufficient information about the medical condition of any child with long term medical needs

2. Check with parents about the medicine that their child needs to take

3. Ensure that you only accept medicines into the setting that have been prescribed by a doctor, dentist, nurse or pharmacist. It is not uncommon for parents to ask for Calpol to be given to their baby for teething reasons, without a prescription. Ensure that a written medication consent form is completed and signed by both the parent and senior member of staff prior to administering Calpol,

showing the agreed dose and how frequently the medicine needs to be given. Parents need to sign the medication form each time any medication is administered. You must not provide Calpol for general use

4. Providers should keep prescribed medicines in a locked non-portable container (except where storage in a fridge is required).

7. Illnesses and injuries

Remember that both the general and specific legal requirements have the force of regulations and therefore must be complied with by all early years providers.

What must you do for the specific requirements?

1. Providers must notify Ofsted and local child protection agencies of any serious accident or injury to, or serious illness of, or the death of, any child whilst in their care, and act on any advice given. An early years provider who, without reasonable excuse, fails to comply with this requirement, commits an offence

2. At least one person who has a current paediatric first aid certificate must be on the premises at all times when children are present. There must be at least one person on outings who has a current paediatric first aid certificate

3. Providers must have a first aid box with appropriate content to meet the needs of children

4. Providers must keep a record of accidents and first aid treatment

5. Providers must inform parents of any accidents or injuries sustained by the child whilst in the care of the providers and of any first aid treatment that was given

6. Providers must discuss with parents the procedure for children who are ill or infectious. This should include the possibility of exclusion as well as the protocol for contacting parents or another adult designated by the parent if a child becomes ill or receives minor injuries whilst in the provider's care.

The Statutory guidance (to which you must give regard) is helpful –

Look on page 26 of the Statutory guidance book. You will find a further point to consider. Think about how you ensure that any animals on the premises are safe to be in the proximity of children and do not pose a health risk.

8. Food and drink

Remember that both the general and specific legal requirements have the force of regulations and therefore must be complied with by all early years providers.

What must you do for the specific requirements?

1. Where children are provided with meals, snacks and drinks, these must be healthy, balanced and nutritious. Those responsible for the preparation and handling of food must be competent to do so. Refer to children aged 16-26 months, physical development; planning and resourcing

2. Fresh drinking water must be available at all times. Refer to 40-60+ months, physical development; planning and resourcing

3. Providers must notify Ofsted of any food poisoning affecting two or more children looked after on the premises. An early years provider who, without reasonable excuse, fails to comply with this requirement, commits an offence.

The Statutory guidance (to which you must give regard) is helpful –

Look on page 27 of the Statutory guidance book. You will find 6 points to consider. Think about how you –

1. provide children with healthy snacks and meals as appropriate

2. inform Ofsted if you believe that any child is suffering from a notifiable disease

3. obtain records from parents from parents about their child's dietary needs. Refer to 22-36 months, physical development; planning and resourcing

4. update your knowledge about food hygiene legislation including registration with the relevant local authority Environmental health Department

5. include food hygiene matters in induction processes

6. how you store packed lunches safely (if provided by parents).

9. Smoking

Remember that both the general and specific legal requirements have the force of regulations and therefore must be complied with by all early years providers.

What must you do for the specific requirements?

1. Providers must ensure that children are in a smoke-free environment

The Statutory guidance (to which you must give regard) is helpful –

Look on page 27 of the Statutory guidance book. You will find a point to consider. Providers should have a no smoking policy which ensures that no one smokes in a room, or outside play area, when children are present or about to be present. If, exceptionally, children are expected to use any space that has been used for smoking, providers should ensure that there is adequate ventilation to clear the atmosphere.

Let's look back to what the general requirements are –

■ The provider must take the necessary steps to safeguard and promote the welfare of children (specific requirements 1-5)

■ The provider must promote the good health of children, take necessary steps to prevent the spread of infection, and take appropriate action when children are ill (specific requirements 6–9)

■ Children's behaviour must be managed effectively and in a manner appropriate for their stage of development and particular individual needs (specific requirements 10).

We have looked at the specific requirements 1-5.

We have looked at the specific requirements 6-9.

The card that broadly links to the general requirements 10 are A Unique Child card 1.3 (Keeping Safe)

Remember that both the general and specific legal requirements have the force of regulations and therefore must be complied with by all early years providers.

You will see that some specific legal requirements have links to the EYFS through the cards and the areas of learning. You may find it helpful to have the cards to refer to as well as Practice Guidance book.

10. Behaviour management

Remember that both the general and specific legal requirements have the force of regulations and therefore must be complied with by all early years providers.

What must you do for the specific requirements?

1. Providers must not give corporal punishment to a child for whom they provide early years provision and, so far as it is reasonably practicable, shall ensure that corporal punishment is not given to any such child by

    a) any person who cares for, or who is in regular contact with, children

    b) any person living or working on the premises

2. An early years provider who, without reasonable excuse, fails to comply with this requirement, commits an offence

3. A person shall not be taken to have given corporal punishment in breach of the above if the action was taken for reasons that include averting an immediate danger of personal injury to, or an immediate danger of death of, any person (including the child)

4. Providers must not threaten corporal punishment, nor use or threaten any form of punishment which could have an adverse impact on the child's well-being

5. Providers must have an effective behaviour management policy, which is adhered to by all members of staff. Refer to children aged 30-50 months, personal, social and emotional development; planning and resourcing.

The Statutory guidance (to which you must give regard) is helpful –

Look on page 28 of the Statutory guidance book. You will find two points to consider.

Physical intervention should only be used to manage a child's behaviour if it is necessary to prevent personal injury to the child, other children or an adult, to prevent serious damage to property, or in what would reasonably be regarded as exceptional circumstances. Any occasion where physical intervention is used to manage a child's behaviour should be recorded and parents should be informed about it on the same day.

Except in childminding settings, a named practitioner should be responsible for behaviour management issues. They should be supported in acquiring the skills to provide guidance to other staff and to access expert advice if ordinary methods are not effective with a particular child.

Other considerations –

Staff need to be aware of your behaviour policy and procedures, if a consistent approach is to be maintained. As with all your policies and procedures, new and existing staff should either have their own copies of the documents, or have access to them for reference. Training and support will be necessary for the staff in managing a wide range of behaviour, and it is likely that your local authority can advise you on what training is available for you in your area. Parents will need to be aware, through you policy statement, how children's behaviour is managed. It is likely that you consider the following, depending on the age and developmental stage of the children –

■ Distraction

■ Explanation

■ Removing the child from the situation.

The key to good management of children's behaviour will lie in your approach to behaviour issues. Consider the following –

Have the staff read and agreed with the behaviour policy? Were they involved in the discussion when the policy was put together, and/or involved in the review?

Do staff praise children's work efforts? This is important; children need their self-esteem building constantly. You should be aiming to encourage children to become confident – to feel good about themselves as people.

Do you allow children need to learn by their mistakes? They should be encouraged to experiment – have a go – and discover why something did not work out. Allow children to make positive relationships with one another. It is sometimes easy for staff to step in too early if there is a dispute. Children need to learn to negotiate and work out problems. Staff may need to step in if the children react aggressively or unkindly.

Do staff have the same consistent approach – thinking about striking a reasonable balance between too much and too little structure? This is not easy, however, the staff need to look at ways in which to achieve the balance in your setting.

Do staff focus on encouraging positive behaviour, rather than focusing on the unacceptable behaviour. Sometimes, it is in the child's interests for the staff to ignore certain behaviour, and engage the child in some other activity, rather than making an issue out of what has just been observed.

Do your staff act as good role models? Children pick up very quickly on adult language and behaviour. How should adults behave? Consider the following –

If the staff respect the children, giving encouragement to trying new skills, the children will respect themselves, and develop a sense of achievement in their own abilities.

If the staff are positive, and tell the children what strengths they have, the children will become more confident in exploring further – attempting greater challenges – a belief in 'I can do this'. Children will attempt new skills, without the fear of failure, if the staff show support for the child's efforts.

Are the staff firm but fair in their approach to the care of the children, recognising that age and developmental stages need to be considered for each child? There is no point in working in the room where children aged 3-5 years are cared for, and expecting the same levels of concentration and understanding from all the children. If you are secure in your knowledge of child development, you will meet the needs of all the children as individuals, and make the appropriate allowances for children when necessary. The EYFS has been designed to assist you with this.

Do staff recognise that all children have needs? These needs include –

■ Love

■ Stability

■ Sense of belonging

■ Security

■ Food

■ Shelter

■ Rest/sleep

■ Consistency

■ Opportunities to learn/develop

■ Companionship.

If the needs are met, why do children behave in unacceptable ways at times?

Children are human beings, with feelings. They have their own views and opinions on issues. They have likes and dislikes. They may be unwell. They may be tired. They may not understand. There may be factors outside of the setting which affect the child's behaviour in the setting, for example, difficulties at home. If there is no consistent routine, a child will not know the boundaries.

All of these points are important, if you are to consider each child as an individual, and understand that there may be good reason for a child to behave in a way that may not be acceptable. There must be a way of dealing with unacceptable behaviour though. How can you address this, keeping the above points in mind?

Firstly, prevention – thinking about what you can do to encourage positive behaviour:

1. Working with parents – clear policies which let parents know what you mean by 'acceptable behaviour', and what measures you have in place for dealing with unacceptable behaviour

2. Explain the 'rules' to the children – what you expect of them in terms of behaviour, in a way in which they will understand

3. Have books available to help children with situations so that they can express their feelings. For example, books that sensitively deal with divorce/separation, death, going into hospital, will assist the child who has anxieties about such situations

4. Maximise the use of your home corner, to allow children to use their imaginations – to 'act out' situations, and explore their feelings

5. Give children time to talk. It is vital in the early years that children are given the opportunity to tell adults about what is happening in their lives – happy and not so happy times – and for the adult to really listen, taking the messages on board to help the child if necessary.

Any of the above will work if you are considering a preventative approach, but we all know that unacceptable behaviour will be seen at times. You preventative measures are needed, but also you have to consider how you are going to deal with the unacceptable behaviour when it happens.

What about the child who continues to act in an unacceptable way? You need to consider the safety aspects for the child, the other children, and the staff too. If a child is going to cause harm to another person, the word 'no' is likely to be used. This is not a problem, unless you do not follow on with an explanation of why you have said 'no'. Children need explanation from the staff – how else will they appreciate why the behaviour was not acceptable? Just saying 'no' is not sufficient to help a child to understand.

Should you punish children? We need to consider the word 'punish'.

The Oxford Dictionary defines 'punish' as – the offender has cause to suffer for his/her offence, inflict a penalty for, treat roughly.

You do need to think about the way in which you will deal with the behaviour, but it must be considered from the point of view of the child's age, the child's developmental stage, the situation when the behaviour was shown, and the cause for the behaviour. Rather than 'punish' a child, think about an age appropriate way of dealing with the situation. Certainly, removing the child from the situation – time out, as some settings refer to this – can be effective, but only for a short time, and with an explanation given to the child as to why they have been removed. Raising your voice, or speaking unkindly to a child is not effective. In fact, it is more likely to give the child a message that this is way that they can treat others. Always be respectful to a child, regardless of the way in which the child has behaved, and let the matter drop when you have dealt with it. Children do not need constant reminders of their unacceptable behaviour.

If parents are to be kept informed of their child's development, you would need to advise them of any difficulties too, either in respect of their general development or behaviour. Parents will need to be advised on any sensitive matter in private – it is not good practice to discuss a child in front of the other children and other parents. You and the parents should be working together for the benefit of each child, looking at ways in which to provide a consistent approach to behaviour management.

Suitable people

The general requirements are –

■ Providers must ensure that adults looking after children, or having unsupervised access to them, are suitable to do so

■ Adults looking after children must have appropriate qualifications, training, skills and knowledge

■ Staffing arrangements must be organised to ensure safety and to meet the needs of the children.

What must you do for the specific requirements?

1. Safe recruitment

2. What Ofsted needs to be notified about

3. Alcohol/other substances

4. Appropriate qualifications, training, skills and knowledge

5. Staffing arrangements.

Remember that both the general and specific legal requirements have the force of regulations and therefore must be complied with by all early years providers.

Ofsted will base the inspections from September 2008 on whether a provider has met the general and specific requirements, and can show that they have given regard to the statutory guidance.

Safe recruitment

What must you do for the specific requirements?

1. Providers must obtain an enhanced Criminal Records Bureau (CRB) Disclosure, which includes a Protection Of Children Act list/List 99 check, in respect of all people who work directly with children or who are likely to have unsupervised access to them

2. Providers must allow only people who have undergone an enhanced CRB check to have unsupervised contact with children on the premises

3. Providers must keep records to demonstrate to Ofsted that the checks have been done, including the number and date of issue of the enhanced CRB Disclosure

4. Providers must have effective systems in place to ensure that practitioners and others likely to have unsupervised access to the children (including those living or working on the premises) are suitable to do so

5. Providers must also have regard to any requirements made under the Safeguarding Vulnerable Groups Act 2006 once these come into force with the intended introduction of a new vetting and barring scheme for those working with children and vulnerable adults from autumn 2008.

The Statutory guidance (to which you must give regard) is helpful –

Look on page 29 of the Statutory guidance book. You will find 6 points to consider. Think about how you –

Make decisions of suitability using evidence from:

■ references

■ full employment history

■ qualifications

■ interviews

■ identity checks

■ any other checks undertaken, for example medical suitability.

Providers should notify all people connected with their provision who work directly with children that they expect them to declare to them all convictions and/or cautions; as well as court orders which may disqualify them from working with children or affect their suitability to do so.

Further information about responsibilities for carrying out CRB checks and about disqualification is provided in the Practice Guidance for the Early Years Foundation Stage.

What does the term 'suitable person' mean?

Ofsted will check that the provider is suitable, by taking up checks and references on the provider. These

checks will also include health and police clearance. Ofsted then leave the responsibility for suitability of other staff employed by the setting to the provider. Safe recruitment is far more than just a police check, which so many providers think is the 'important' check.

Your initial views on any person are formed when you first meet. You may have had a conversation on the phone prior to the meeting/interview, however, you will be determining the person's suitability in a number of ways –

■ The interview

■ The person's C.V. Full information should be available so that you can be sure you have all the details of work history, with no gaps

■ Qualifications

■ Age and experience

■ Health declaration

■ Police clearance.

When staff are being recruited, providers have a responsibility to ensure that the staff are suitable. Look at your recruitment procedures – do they reflect how you take on new staff? Do your application forms state clearly the post that is being applied for, with a full and clear job description? Does the wording in your advertisements allow for equality of opportunity? Do you have an induction package for new staff, so that they are aware of all of your policies and procedures?

The terms for employment (contract) for any new member of staff should be clear. Other than the place of employment and job title, you should state the pay conditions, hours of work and notice period. Be clear about sickness pay and holiday entitlements, in addition to clear disciplinary and grievance procedures. If a probationary period is offered, you would provide a contract to reflect this, with a permanent contract offered at the end of that time. Even if the position is temporary, a contract is advisable.

A contract and induction package means that any new member of staff will be clear about their individual role and job responsibility. The contract will need to be signed as an agreement, and it is advisable to ask the new staff member to sign their name to the information given to them in the induction package, as a record that they have read, understood and agree to follow the policies and procedures. Some settings issue the induction package to all staff as it is updated, so that everyone is in agreement on a consistent approach to the policies of the setting. Employment issues are important, and most settings need advice at some stage on how to deal with specific queries.

You also need to consider other people working in your setting, such as those on work experience, or volunteers, to ensure that they are fully supported whilst they are with your setting.

Most providers do not have health backgrounds, and would not necessarily know what to look for. A suggestion is to consider devising your own health declaration form. New staff, and even existing staff could annually declare that they are in good health. Your disciplinary procedures could come into force if you then had cause to question the signed declaration.

Taking up references is very important – preferably in writing. This will show that you have taken every opportunity to check out your staff. Part of your recruitment procedure should show that you offer positions for a probationary period, during which time, you should try to get to know the new staff member, and offer support as the probationary time goes by. If, at the end of this time, you are happy with the person, you may choose to offer a permanent post. However, if things have not worked out, you may decide to either extend the probationary period, or tell the person that you will not be able to offer them a permanent post.

Providers who employ a person to manage the setting need to be certain that they are suitable before they are left in charge. It is the provider's responsibility to ensure that the setting is in safe hands. This is more than just a qualification issue. The person in charge must be competent in their work, and be able to demonstrate a clear understanding of the EYFS.

What Ofsted needs to be notified about

What must you do for the specific requirements?

Providers must notify Ofsted of –

1. any change of provider or person with direct responsibility for early years provision

2. any proposal of childminders to employ an assistant to look after children

3. any change of persons of 16 years or over living or working on childminding premises

4. any proposal to change the hours during which childcare is provided which will entail the provision of overnight care

5. any change to the premises from which childcare is provided which may affect the space available to children and the quality of childcare available to them

6. any change in their name or address

7. any change in the name or registered number of a company, or any change in the name or registration number of a charity

8. any change in the address of premises on which childcare is provided

9. any criminal offence committed by the registered provider after the time of registration.

An early years provider who, without reasonable excuse, fails to comply with this requirement, commits an offence.

The Statutory guidance (to which you must give regard) is helpful –

Look on page 30 of the Statutory guidance book. You will find 2 points to consider. You should advise Ofsted -

Where there is a change of provider or person in charge, or any change in persons of 16 years or over living or working on childminding premises, the information provided should be the new person's date of birth, name, any former names or aliases and home address.

Where accessible individual records are kept on the premises containing

the name and address of the staff members, any volunteers and committee members, and information about recruitment, training and qualifications.

Alcohol/other substances

What must you do for the specific requirements?

1. When working directly with children, practitioners must not be under the influence of alcohol or any other substance, which may affect their ability to care for children.

The Statutory guidance (to which you must give regard) is helpful –

Look on page 30 of the Statutory guidance book. You will find a point to consider.

Practitioners taking medication which they believe may affect their ability to care for children should seek medical advice and only work directly with children if that advice is that the medication is unlikely to impair their ability to look after children.

Another consideration -

If it is suspected that a member of staff is under the influence of alcohol or any other substance, the provider should take immediate steps to safeguard the children. This may mean removing the member of staff from areas where the children are being cared for, and asking the member of staff to leave the premises. You may ask the member of staff to get a letter from their doctor, to establish their suitability in terms of their health, to be in the vicinity of young children.

Let's refer back to what the general requirements are –

■ Providers must ensure that adults looking after children, or having unsupervised access to them, are suitable to do so

■ Adults looking after children must have appropriate qualifications, training, skills and knowledge

■ Staffing arrangements must be organised to ensure safety and to meet the needs of the children.

We have looked at the first requirement.

The second general requirement is –

2. Adults looking after children must have appropriate qualifications, training, skills and knowledge.

Remember that both the general and specific legal requirements have the force of regulations and therefore must be complied with by all early years providers.

What must you do for the specific requirements?

1. Childminders must have attended a training course within six months of registration and must hold a current paediatric first aid certificate at the point of registration. First aid training must be approved by the local authority and consistent with the guidance set out in the Practice Guidance for the Early Years Foundation Stage (page 21)

2. All supervisors and managers must hold a full and relevant level 3 (as defined by the Children's Workforce Development Council (CWDC)) and half of all other staff must hold a full and relevant level 2 (as defined by CWDC).

The Statutory guidance (to which you must give regard) is helpful –

Look on page 31 of the Statutory guidance book. You will find 7 points to consider.

How do you -

■ ensure, if you are a childminder, that you have attended a training course to familiarise yourself with the EYFS? Wherever possible, childminders should have attended a training course prior to or shortly after registration. The training should be approved by the local authority and provide support for childminders (new and existing) in meeting and putting into practice the requirements of the EYFS. Childminders are accountable for, and supervise the work of, any assistant. The childminder should be satisfied that they are competent in the areas of work undertaken. First aid training needs to be updated every three years for all practitioners

■ check that the manager has at least two years' experience of working in an early years setting, or have at least two years' other suitable experience?

■ ensure that all practitioners in your setting have a clear understanding of their roles and responsibilities?

■ support staff in improving their qualification levels? In particular, those staff with no qualifications should be supported in obtaining a relevant qualification at a minimum of a full and relevant level 2 (as defined by CWDC)

■ provide a comprehensive induction training for new staff to help them understand how the provision operates and their role within it? Induction training should include matters such as evacuation procedures and child protection and health and safety issues

■ organise regular staff appraisals to identify the training needs of staff? A programme of continuing professional development should be applied so that these needs are met

■ encourage staff to use training made available by the local authority and other sources?

Let's refer back to what the general requirements are –

■ Providers must ensure that adults looking after children, or having unsupervised access to them, are suitable to do so

■ Adults looking after children must have appropriate qualifications, training, skills and knowledge

■ Staffing arrangements must be organised to ensure safety and to meet the needs of the children.

We have looked at the first two requirements.

The third general requirement is –

3. Staffing arrangements must be organised to ensure safety and to meet the needs of the children.

Remember that both the general and specific legal requirements have the force of regulations and therefore must be complied with by all early years providers.

What must you do for the specific requirements?

1. Providers must meet the requirements for adult:child ratios.

These are set out in Appendix 2 of the Statutory book on pages 49-51

2. During breaks, or at times when teachers are undertaking preparation, planning and assessment, and are out of the classroom/not interacting directly with the children, the ratios must be adjusted accordingly. Refer to children aged 30-50 months, personal, social and emotional development; planning and resourcing

3. In registered group settings there must be a named deputy who is able to take charge in the absence of the manager

4. For childminders providing overnight care, required ratios continue to apply. The children must be close by and within easy hearing distance (this may be via a monitor)

5. For other settings providing overnight care, the ratios set out in these requirements continue to apply. At least one member of staff must be awake at all times.

The Statutory guidance (to which you must give regard) is helpful –

Look on page 32 of the Statutory guidance book. You will find 8 points to consider.

Children should be supervised at all times, with staffing arrangements organised to meet the individual needs of all children.

Exceptions to the ratios requirements should only be made in limited circumstances, such as when the children are sleeping or resting. In these circumstances all the adults need not be present in the room with the children, but should be available nearby on the premises should they be needed.

Providers should put in place contingency arrangements for staff absences and emergencies. Refer to children aged birth – 11 months, knowledge and understanding of the world; effective practice. Refer to children aged 30-50 months, personal, social and emotional development; effective practice. When there is staff absence or an emergency occurs suitable arrangements might include drawing on a pool of suitable staff, re-grouping of children, re-organising rooms and

activities and re-deploying other suitable staff. When such disruptions occur there should continue to be a consistent experience for the child.

Where children in nursery classes and reception classes attend school for longer than the normal school day, in provision run directly by the governing body or the proprietor, we recommend that outside the school day the adult: child ratio is held at 1:8 with at least one member of staff holding a full and relevant level 3 (as defined by CWDC) and half of all others holding a full and relevant level 2 (as defined by CWDC).

Staff/volunteers/students under the age of 17 cannot count towards the ratio and should be supervised at all times. Individuals aged 17 and over who are on long-term placements may be included in the ratios if the provider is satisfied they are competent and responsible.

Volunteers/committee members are given full information and guidance on their roles and responsibilities.

Some schools may choose to mix their reception classes with groups of younger children, in which case they should use their discretion in establishing ratios for these mixed groups based on the EYFS welfare requirements (that is, 1:30 for the reception group and 1:13, 1:8 and so on for the younger children). This applies whether the pre-school element is provided directly by the school or in partnership through a PVI provider. However, in exercising this discretion the school, and any partner provider, must comply with the statutory requirements relating to the education of children of compulsory school age children and infant class sizes. At all times it is necessary to meet the needs of individual children and it may be appropriate to exceed these minimum requirements. Where a school operates in partnership with a PVI pre-school provider both parties will assume shared responsibility for meeting the ratios in the amalgamated setting.

Examples of how these mixed-age groups may work in practice are set out in the *Practice Guidance for the Early Years Foundation Stage.*

There has been much debate about the requirements for adult:child ratios for children aged three plus. The Primary National Strategy states ' that there is no evidence that allowing

providers to apply a ratio of 1 adult to 13 children will put children in danger. The ratio applies to children aged over 3 years and only when a teacher, Early Year Professional Status or a person with another suitable level 6 qualification is present and interacting directly with the children. At other times, providers would have to continue to meet the existing 1:8 ratio requirement. Many nursery schools already have a ratio of 1:13 and there is no evidence to suggest that children who attend those schools are at greater risk than those attending other types of setting. Moreover, ratio requirements represent minimum levels below which provision will not legally be allowed to fall. We want to encourage more settings to employ more highly qualified staff, and this will encourage them to do so'.

This statement has not satisfied everyone. Some practitioners have expressed their disappointment that a Level 3 qualification is no longer deemed 'enough' to be responsible for groups of children, but only as a 'support' to the teacher, unless the children are in the setting before 8am and after 4pm. The debate will undoubtedly continue.

Suitable premises, environment and equipment

The general requirement is –

Outdoor and indoor spaces, furniture, equipment and toys must be safe and suitable for their purpose.

This requirement links to card 3.3 Enabling Environments, The learning Environment.

What must you do for the specific requirements?

1. Risk assessment

2. Premises

3. Organising the premises and equipment.

Remember that both the general and specific legal requirements have the force of regulations and therefore must be complied with by all early years providers.

Ofsted will base the inspections from September 2008 on whether a provider has met the general and specific requirements, and can show that they have given regard to the statutory guidance.

Risk assessment

What must you do for the specific requirements?

1. The provider must conduct a risk assessment and review it regularly – at least once a year or more frequently where the need arises. Refer to children aged 40-60+ months, physical development; planning and resourcing. Refer to children aged 22-36 months, physical development; planning and resourcing

2. The risk assessment must identify aspects of the environment that need to be checked on a regular basis: providers must maintain a record of these particular aspects and when and by whom they have been checked. Providers must determine the regularity of these checks according to their assessment of the significance of individual risks

3. The provider must take all reasonable steps to ensure that hazards to children – both indoors and outdoors – are kept to a minimum.

The Statutory guidance (to which you must give regard) is helpful –

Look on page 33 of the Statutory guidance book. You will find 3 points to consider –

■ The risk assessment should cover anything with which a child may come into contact

■ The premises and equipment should be clean, and providers should be aware of the requirements of health and safety legislation (including hygiene requirements). This should include informing and keeping staff up-to-date

■ A health and safety policy should be in place, which includes procedures for identifying, reporting and dealing with accidents, hazards and faulty equipment.

Premises

What must you do for the specific requirements?

1. Providers must inform Ofsted of any significant changes or events relating to the premises on which childcare is provided

2. Significant changes or events which must be reported to Ofsted include

   a) significant changes to the premises, for example structural alterations or an extension

   b) something which adversely affects the smooth running of the provision over a sustained period of time

   c) changes to the outside of the premises such as adding a pond or taking down fencing.

Providers must take reasonable steps to ensure the safety of children, staff and others on the premises in the case of fire, and must have a clearly defined procedure for the emergency evacuation of the premises.

Providers must have appropriate fire detection and control equipment (for example, fire alarms, smoke detectors, fire extinguishers and fire blankets) which are in working order.

The Statutory guidance (to which you must give regard) is helpful –

Look on page 34 of the Statutory guidance book. You will find 4 points to consider –

■ Where children stay overnight, it may be appropriate for the Fire Safety Officer to inspect the sleeping area

■ Staff should understand their roles and responsibilities in the event of a fire

■ Fire exits should be clearly identifiable; fire doors should be free from obstructions and easily opened from the inside

■ Regular evacuation drills should be carried out and details recorded in a fire log book of any problems encountered and how they were resolved.

Organising the premises and equipment

What must you do for the specific requirements?

1. In registered provision, providers must meet the following space requirements:

■ children under two years: 3.5 m^2 per child

■ two year olds: 2.5 m^2 per child

■ children aged three to five years: 2.3 m^2 per child.

2. The provider must ensure that, so far as is reasonable, the facilities, equipment and access to the premises are suitable for children with disabilities

3. The premises must be for the sole use of the provision during the hours of operation

4. The provider must carry and display public liability insurance for the provision.

The Statutory guidance (to which you must give regard) is helpful –

Look on page 35 of the Statutory guidance book. You will find 15 points to consider –

The premises should be clean, adequately ventilated and well lit. Daylight should be the main source of light. Where, in exceptional circumstances this is not possible, the provider should ensure that lighting is of good quality and children have adequate access to daylight.

Calculations of available indoor space should be based on the net or useable areas of the rooms used by the children (that is, not including storage areas, thoroughfares, dedicated staff areas, cloakrooms, utility rooms, kitchens and toilets).

Wherever possible, there should be access to an outdoor play area, and this is the expected norm for providers. In provision where outdoor play space cannot be provided, outings should be planned and taken on a daily basis (unless circumstances make this inappropriate, for example unsafe weather conditions).

There should be adequate space to give scope for free movement and well-spread activities. Refer to ages 8-20 months, physical development; planning and resourcing.

In addition to the area per child stated in the requirements, there should be space within the premises to store children's records, toys and personal belongings. There should also be sufficient space to use and store any specialist equipment needed, for example, by disabled children. This equipment should be quickly and easily accessible by staff at the provision so that it can be used by those children whenever it is required. Security should be considered.

Rooms should be maintained at a temperature, which ensures the comfort of the children and staff, including non-mobile children.

Except in childminding settings, there should be a separate baby room for children under the age of two, but they should be able to have contact with older children and be transferred to the older age-group after the age of 18 months or as appropriate for their individual stage of development.

Provision should be made (space or partitioned area) for children who wish to relax, play quietly or sleep, equipped with appropriate furniture. This may be converted from normal play space providing children can rest and/or sleep safely without disturbance. Each child should have their own bed linen, flannel, and hairbrush if they are used (these may be provided by parents or providers). Sleeping children should be frequently checked.

Where children are staying overnight, they should each have a suitable bed or cot and clean bedding.

There should be an area which is adequately equipped to provide healthy meals, snacks and drinks for the children as necessary. Ideally, the provision will have a full kitchen. Where this is not possible, appropriate alternative arrangements should be made for the hygienic preparation and storage of food and drinks.

There should be suitable facilities for the hygienic preparation of babies' feeds if necessary. Suitable sterilisation equipment is used for the sterilisation of babies' feeding equipment and dummies.

There should be at least one toilet and one hand basin for every ten children over the age of two. Except in childminding settings, there should normally be separate toilet facilities for adults. There should be adequate washing and toileting facilities for children who stay overnight.

There should be suitable hygienic changing facilities for changing any children who are in nappies and providers should ensure that an adequate supply of clean bedding, towels, spare clothes and any other necessary items are always available. Children should not be allowed access to any laundry facilities that are provided on site.

Where the early years provision takes place in a communal building such as a community centre or village hall, the part of the premises used by the early years provision should be for the sole use of the provision during the hours of operation. Ideally, the premises should have their own kitchen and toilet facilities but, where this is not possible, the provider should take steps to ensure that other users do not have a negative impact on the quality or safety of provision.

There should be an area where confidential information and necessary records can be kept and where staff may talk to parents confidentially. Staff should have a room or area available for breaks, away from areas being used by children.

Refer to card 3.1 Enabling Environments, The Learning Environment. This will help you to focus on the emotional environment, the outdoor environment, effective practice, challenges and dilemmas and how you can reflect on your practice. For example, under this heading –

■ emotional environment is created by all the people in the setting, but

adults have to ensure that it is warm and accepting of everyone.

■ Adults need to empathise with children and support their emotions

■ When children feel confident in the environment they are willing to try things out, knowing that effort is valued

■ When children know that their feelings are accepted they learn to express them, confident that adults will help them with how they are feeling.

Organisation

The general requirements is –

■ Providers must plan and organise their systems to ensure that every child receives an enjoyable and challenging learning and development experience that is tailored to meet their individual needs.

The cards that broadly link to the general requirements are –

■ A Unique Child card 1.1 (Child development)

■ Enabling Environments card 3.3 (The learning environment) and Learning and Development card 4.2 (Active learning).

Remember that both the general and specific legal requirements have the force of regulations and therefore must be complied with by all early years providers.

Ofsted will base the inspections from September 2008 on whether a provider has met the general and specific requirements, and can show that they have given regard to the statutory guidance.

What must you do for the specific requirements?

1. Providers must have effective systems to ensure that the individual needs of all children are met. Refer to children aged 40-60+ months, physical development; effective practice. Refer to card Positive Relationships 2.4 Key Person

2. Each child must be assigned a key person. In childminding settings, the childminder is the key person

Refer to children aged birth – 11 months, personal, social and emotional development; planning and resourcing

3. Providers must promote equality of opportunity and anti-discriminatory practice and must ensure that every child is included and not disadvantaged because of ethnicity, culture or religion, home language, family background, learning difficulties or disabilities, gender or ability

4. Providers must ensure that there is a balance of adult-led and freely chosen or child-initiated activities, delivered through indoor and outdoor play. Refer to children aged 40-60 + months, personal, social and emotional development; planning and resourcing

5. Providers must undertake sensitive observational assessment in order to plan to meet young children's individual needs. Refer to children aged 22-36 months, communication, language and literacy; effective practice. Refer to children aged 22-36 months, personal, social and emotional development; planning and resourcing. Refer to children aged 8-20 months, knowledge and understanding of the world; effective practice

6. Providers must plan and provide experiences which are appropriate to each child's stage of development as they progress towards the early learning goals. Refer the children aged 30-50 months, physical development; planning and resourcing.

The Statutory guidance (to which you must give regard) is helpful –

Look on page 37 of the Statutory guidance book. You will find 3 points to consider –

■ The key person should help the baby or child to become familiar with the provision and to feel confident and safe within it, developing a genuine bond with the child (and the child's parents) and offering a settled, close relationship

■ The key person should meet the needs of each child in their care and respond sensitively to their feelings, ideas and behaviour, talking to parents to make sure that the child

is being cared for appropriately for each family. Refer to children aged birth –11 months, personal, social and emotional development, effective practice

■ Practitioners should value linguistic diversity and provide opportunities for children to develop and use their home language in their play and learning. This is part of the respect for each child's cultural background that is central in all early years provision. Alongside support in the home language, practitioners should provide a range of meaningful contexts in which children have opportunities to develop English. As they move into the Key Stage 1 curriculum, English will be crucial as the language they use to access learning. Refer to children aged 30-50 months, communication, language and literacy; planning and resourcing. Refer to children aged 30- 50 months, personal, social and emotional development; effective practice.

Documentation

The general requirement is –

■ Providers must maintain records, policies and procedures required for the safe and efficient management of the settings and to meet the needs of the children.

Remember that both the general and specific legal requirements have the force of regulations and therefore must be complied with by all early years providers.

Ofsted will base the inspections from September 2008 on whether a provider has met the general and specific requirements, and can show that they have given regard to the statutory guidance.

What must you do for the specific requirements?

1. Data

2. Provider's records.

Data

What must you do for the specific requirements?

Providers must record the following information for each child in their care:

■ full name

- date of birth

- the name and address of every parent and carer who is known to the provider

- which of these parents or carers the child normally lives with

- emergency contact details of the parents and carers.

Providers must record and submit the following information to their local authority about individual children receiving the free entitlement to early years provision as part of the Early Years Census:

- full name

- date of birth

- address

- gender

- ethnicity. This data item can be collected on a voluntary basis. A child's ethnicity should only be recorded where parents have identified the ethnicity of their child themselves

- special educational needs status

- the number of funded hours taken up during the census week

- total number of hours (funded and unfunded) taken up at the setting during the census week.

For maintained and independent schools, these requirements are in addition to the requirements of the Pupil Registration Regulations 2006.

The Statutory guidance (to which you must give regard) is helpful –

Look on pages 38 and 39 of the Statutory guidance book. You will find some further points to consider –

Ethnicity, where collected, should be recorded according to the following categories:

White – British

- Irish

- Traveller of Irish Heritage

- Gypsy/Roma

- Any other white background.

Mixed – White and Black Caribbean

- White and Black African

- White and Asian

- Any other mixed background.

Asian or Asian British

- Indian

- Pakistani

- Bangladeshi

- Any other Asian background.

Black or Black British

- Caribbean

- African

- Any other Black background.

Chinese

Any other ethnic background

A child's learning difficulties and disabilities status should be recorded according to the following categories:

- no special educational need;

- Early Years Action/School Action;

- Early Years Action Plus/School Action Plus;

- statement.

Providers should refer to the SEN Code of Practice for an explanation of the terms used above.

Provider's Records

What must you do for the specific requirements?

1. Providers must keep the following information and documentation:

- name, home address and telephone number of the provider and any other person living or employed on the premises (this requirement does not apply to childminders)

- name, home address and telephone number of anyone else who will regularly be in unsupervised contact with the children attending the early years provision

- a daily record of the names of the children looked after on the premises, their hours of attendance and the names of the children's key workers

- providers must display their certificate of registration and show it to parents on request

- a record of the risk assessment clearly stating when it was carried out, by whom, date of review and any action taken following a review or incident.

Records must be easily accessible and available for inspection by Ofsted (with prior agreement by Ofsted, these may be kept off the premises).

Where Ofsted notifies providers in advance of the period in which an inspection will take place, this information must be passed on to parents. (Section 6 of the Education Act 2005 places an equivalent requirement on schools.)

Providers must ensure that copies of the inspection report are provided to all parents. (Sections 5 and 15 of the Education Act 2005 place an equivalent duty on schools.)

The Statutory guidance (to which you must give regard) is helpful –

Providers should be aware of their responsibilities under the Data Protection Act 1998 and Freedom of Information Act 2000.

Records relating to individual children should be retained for a reasonable period of time (for example three years) after the children have left the provision.

There should be a suitable secure area for the storage of confidential information. Records on staff and children should only be accessible to those who have a right or professional need to see them.

All staff should be aware of the need for confidentiality.

The following list of resources will assist you in working with children in the Early Years Foundation Stage. Further detail on these resources can be found on the EYFS CD-ROM.

Useful Resources

- Building For Sure Start

- Designing School Grounds

- Building Bulletin 99 : Briefing Framework for Primary School Projects

- Developing Accessible Play Space

- The Education (School Premises) Regulations 1999

- The Management of Health and Safety at Work Regulations 1992

- The Workplace (Health, Safety and Welfare) Regulations 1992

- Explanatory Notes to Care Standards Act 2000

- The Regulatory Reform (Fire Safety) Order 2005

- Notification of Infectious Diseases List

- Working Together to Safeguard Children

- Health and Safety of Pupils on Educational Visits

- The Food Standards Agency

- Guidance on Managing Medicines in Schools and Early Years Settings

- Guidance on First Aid for Schools

- The Health and Safety Executive

- Useful Guidance on Accidents Books

- Guidance on Infection Control in Schools and Nurseries

- Health Protection Agency

- Guidance About Nutrition for Young Children

- The CRB Code of practice and Explanatory Guide

- Common Hazardous Plants

- Introduction to Health and Safety

- Social and Emotional Aspects of Learning (SEAL) Programme

- Record keeping and Recording Assessments

- Common Assessment Framework (CAF)

- Disability Discrimination Act 1995

- Data Protection Act 1998

- Freedom of Information Act 2000

- Childcare Act 2006

- Assessment and Reporting Arrangements (ARA's)

- Criminal Records Bureau

- Vetting and Barring

You can order most publications through the DfES publications line on 0845 6022260. This phone line is still available, although the DfES no longer exists as one department.

In June 2007, the Department for Education and Skills (DfES) was replaced by two new departments. These are –

- Department for Children, Schools and Families (DCSF)

- Department for Innovation, Universities and Skills (DIUS)

The Department for Children, Schools and Families will be leading on improving the outcomes for children, including work on children's health and child poverty.

This new department can be contacted in the following ways –

- DCSF
  Website www.dcsf.gov.uk
  Telephone 0870 000 2288
  Fax 01928 794 248